The Oxfordshire Brewer

Preface

Acknowledgements

This booklet is based on a research project carried out by Oxfordshire Museum Services between 1981 and 1983, and owes a great deal to the helpful advice and information given by many individuals and institutions. In particular we should like to thank the remaining brewery companies themselves — Brakspear's, Hook Norton, Morland's, Morrell's and Halls; the Oxford colleges, particularly the Queen's College and Magdalen College; the staff of the Bodleian Library, of the Oxfordshire County Libraries and the County Record Offices of Oxfordshire and Berkshire; among individuals Cynthia Bradford, Joan Brasnett, Vernon Brooke, Judi Caton, Carol Cutler, Sue Etchells, Susannah Everett, J. R. Gray, Ival Hornbrook, R. Howe, D. Kelsey, Carol Nightingale, John Steane, Dr Kate Tiller, Simon Wiggins, and members of the Adderbury Local History Class 1980-81 must be acknowledged for their kind contributions. Too numerous to mention individually are the many owners of former brewing and malting sites who generously allowed access to their premises.

The detailed records of the research project are deposited in the Sites and Monuments Record at the County Museum, Woodstock, where they are available for consultation.

For the provision of illustrations and for permission to reproduce material, grateful acknowledgement is made to: Ashmolean Museum, page 13; Bodleian Library, pages 7 and 36 (upper); W. H. Brakspear and Sons, pages 25, 28, 33; Hook Norton Brewery Co., pages 30 and 34; Mr D. Lewis, inside front cover; Morland and Co., pages 22, 23 and 32; Morrell's Brewery (front cover); Oxfordshire County Libraries, pages 35 and 36 (lower).

Other photographs are in the possession of Oxfordshire Museum Services; all maps are by James Bond.

This excellent publication — at once entertaining, wide-ranging, scholarly and, in effect, a history of the English brewing industry in little — provides a permanent record of the exhibition on the history of brewing in Oxfordshire which was organized by the Department of Museum Services of the county in 1983/4. It is a worthy evocation of the history of brewing, which is an archetypal local industry throughout England, for which doubtless every other English county could produce a similar account (for brewing and associated malting if not for hop-growing). Every mode of organization and production finds its place: medieval monastic brewing in Abingdon, college brewhouses in Oxford, household brewing across the county whether in farm or mansion, brewing publicans, small village brewers and the larger public (or 'common') brewers in the towns.

Twenty years ago this local microcosm of a national story would have been read as entirely 'dead' history. Indeed, if trends current then of increasing scale, national branding and concentration of production had continued for the future as they had been progressing in the recent past, there would by now have been no beer production left in the county to record; only a little local distribution, some bottling perhaps — and consumption. But, unusually for the evolution of trends in industry, history is being re-enacted in the brewing industry, if on a small scale. The reader will thus discover in these pages a current revival of brewing publicans, the expansion of local specialised brewers, the renewal of local names and companies (even if now as subsidiaries of national firms), a flourishing country brewery at Hook Norton, three town breweries still operating, large industrial maltings at Abingdon and Wallingford, a brew-house re-born in the middle of Oxford at Gloucester Green (no less!) and even a hop-garden at Kingston Bagpuize belonging to Morlands of Abingdon — and all this apart from the beer-kit resurrection of truly domestic household brewing. No college ales are still brewed, alas, and all these historic survivals and revivals, of course, co-exist with the great onward march of lager and other national and international brands. But the new lives happily with the old and so much of the history of brewing is alive and well in Oxfordshire. This book records it for all citizens, exactly as a county museum's service ought to do.

Peter Mathias (**Chichele Professor of Economic History, All Souls College, Oxford**)

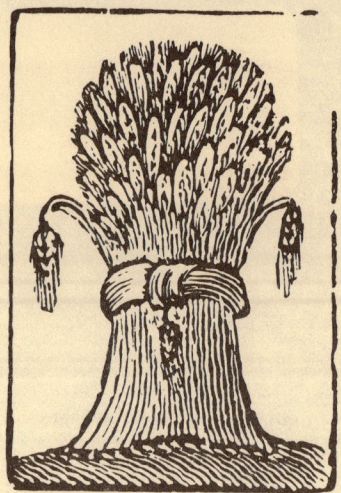

The Barley Sheaf, woodcut by Thomas Bewick.

The Origins of Brewing

The basis of brewing is malt — grain which has been partially germinated and then dried. The sugar contained in the malt is dissolved in water and converted through fermentation into alchohol; the malt also imparts flavour and colour. Pliny the Elder observed that 'the western nations intoxicate themselves by means of moistened grain' and malting and brewing were widespread long before the rise of Roman power. The basic process of malting was known in Mesopotamia before the fifth millenium BC, and it is probable that by about 2,000 BC a knowledge of brewing had been disseminated throughout north-west Europe and into Britain.

Ale is mentioned as a food-rent in the laws of Ine, the late seventh century king of Wessex, and by the Middle Ages there is ample evidence of it being brewed in almost every village. In the centuries that followed, brewing grew into an important trade in nearly every part of Britain. In Oxfordshire, with its ready supplies of malting barley, brewing became one of the county's leading industries, and the brewery and malthouse were common sights in all the towns and in many of the villages.

Ale in the Middle Ages: 'the naturell drynke for Englishmen'

Writers of the sixteenth and seventeenth centuries distinguished between 'ale' and 'beer'. 'Beer' originally meant a drink flavoured by hops; it was virtually unknown in Britain before about 1400, and was not widely accepted until well into the sixteenth century. The medieval drink was ale and it was drunk universally, by all classes, at all times of day and by men, women and children. Because it was boiled, and contained preservatives, it was safer than most of the water available in the Middle Ages. It was quite unlike any modern beer. When brewed only with grain it tasted thick, sticky and rather sweet. A variety of herbs and spices might be added to clarify, season and preserve it or to disguise its taste when it had turned sour. In addition to native wild and garden plants, exotic substances were used — Chaucer records the use of nutmeg, already being brought from the far east. Other common additives included bog myrtle or sweet gale, ground ivy, betony, yarrow, tansy, ling, wormwood, watercress, juniper, rosemary, sage, hyssop, coriander, mace, cinnamon and long pepper. Combinations of herbs used for flavouring ale were called 'gruits' and some continued to be used by domestic brewers in remoter areas well into the present century. Even in Oxford, St John's College was making payments for wormwood and ground ivy in the 1740s and ground ivy beer continued to be brewed for Ascension Day perambulations until recent times. Quite apart from the variety contributed by added flavourings, several different types and grades of ale are recorded during the Middle Ages.

The Anglo-Saxon sources distinguish between the lighter, clearer English Ale and the Welsh Ale or *cwrw*, a heavy glutinous liquid with a smoky taste derived from the roasting of the malt barley. The laws of Ine state that the food-rent of ten hides should include twelve 'ambers' of Welsh ale and thirty of clear ale, plus given quantities of honey, butter, cheeses, livestock and fish. A charter of King Offa of Mercia, dating from c. 793-6, records that the rent of an estate at Westbury-on-Trym included two tuns of pure ale, a coomb of mild ale and a coomb of Welsh ale.

Welsh ale retained its character and popularity in the western parts of Britain into the late eighteenth century. The Cornish ale mocked and denigrated by Andrew Boorde in 1547 was probably similar:

'Iche cam a Cornyshe man, ale che can brew;
It wyll mak one to kacke, also to spew;
It is thycke and smoky, and also it is thyn;
It is lyke wash as pygges had wrestled thryn'.

Yarrow and sage, two of the many herbs used to flavour ale during the Middle Ages. From John Gerard's 'Herbal', 1633.

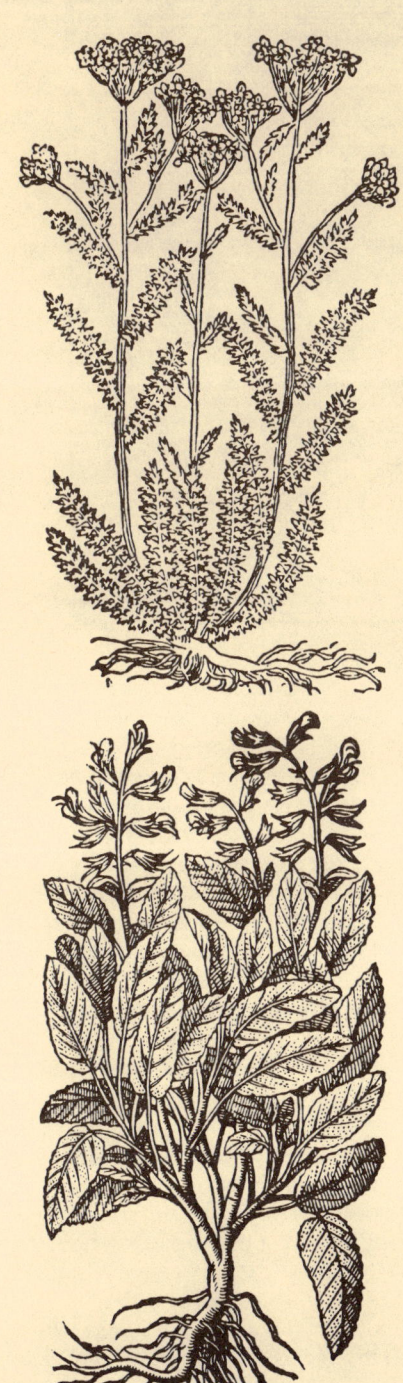

Welsh ale sweetened with honey, known as *bragot,* is mentioned in the early tenth century Welsh laws. Spices from the far east such as cinnamon and galingale (a type of ginger) were also added when they became available later in the Middle Ages. In England it was sometimes drunk in mid-Lent on Bragget Sunday.

Fourteenth century English sources frequently refer to two or three grades of ale, the strongest coming from the first strainings of the mash-vat, with weaker 'small' ales from the later washings. Langland in *Piers Plowman* distinguishes not only between good ale and small or thin ale, but also between cheap country ale and the best brown ale sold in the towns. There was also a distinction between the *bright ale* of wealthier establishments, which had been allowed to stand for a long time to allow its dregs to settle, and Langland's *pudding ale,* a thick drink of the poor in which the dregs had not had time to settle out. Later in the Middle Ages some extra-strong twice-brewed ales and *huffcaps* were being produced.

Beer and Hops: a Foreign Innovation

By the fourteenth century hopped beer had become an important commodity in Flanders, and it was from here that it was first introduced into Britain. Flemish and Dutch brewers were settling in London by about 1400 and were still prominent in the London brewing industry a century or more later. The cultivation of hops began on a small scale in south-east England at about the same time. The early beer brewers were not subjected to any controls, but in 1441 they were brought under an assize. The conditions were similar to those under which ale brewers worked — the malt was to be of good sound corn, either barley and oats or barley and wheat, which should not be too dry or rotten or full of the worms called 'wifles'; the hops were not to be old or rotten; the beer was not to leave the brewery until eight days after brewing, and prices were strictly regulated.

There was some initial resistance to the bitter flavour of hopped beer even in London. Early in the fifteenth century the Brewer's Company of the City of London petitioned the Lord Mayor that ale should be made only from 'licour, malt and yeste', and that 'hoppes, herbs or other like things' should not be permitted in it. Henry VIII forbade his own brewers to add hops or brimstone to the ale of the royal household. Although hopped beer had achieved some popularity in London by the later fifteenth century, resistance in the provinces was stronger. Andrew Boorde in 1548 still regarded ale as the 'naturell drynke' for Englishmen and thought beer was fit only for Dutchmen — yet, 'nowe of later dayes it is moche used in England to the detryment of many Englyshe men; . . . specyally it kylleth them the which be troubled with the colycke and the stone and the strangulation; for the drynke is a cold drynke; yet it doth make a man fat, and doth inflate the bely." Slowly, however, the bitter taste came to be appreciated and the better keeping properties of hopped beer encouraged its adoption at the expense of ale. By the later sixteenth century almost all ales were beginning to be lightly hopped in order to keep better. William Harrison's view, in his 'Description of England', illustrates the extent to which tastes had changed by 1577: having accepted the taste of hopped beer, he speaks with some repugnance of the thick old ale, 'an old and sick man's drink', which remained popular only with a few.

3

The Household Brewer

'The Brewer', woodcut by John Trusler, 1791.

Brewing in the Small Household

To the peasant farmer of the early Middle Ages, growing barley for malting and brewing ale for the family were necessary parts of the planning of the farming year. When a surplus of barley was available, ale sold to neighbours provided a useful supplement to household income. Ale appears to have had a greater internal sale than any other commodity produced on the average manor and it is only when it was brewed to sell that the peasant brewers became subject to the assize of ale and thus enter the historical record.

The account rolls of the Earldom of Cornwall's extensive honours of Wallingford and St. Valery in Oxfordshire record the receipt of many payments for breaches of the assize of ale in 1296-7. At least three or four brewers appear in almost every village and in some places considerable numbers were listed — 43 at Chalgrove, 29 at Watlington, 24 at Beckley. The occasional use of 'brewer' and 'brewster' as surnames, for example by Felicia *braciatrice* of Beckley, suggests the emergence of some specialist producers. In the later Middle Ages there is increasing evidence for a few individuals beginning to operate on a larger scale. At the Cuxham court in 1341, Robert Oldman paid toll for brewing on ten occasions, whereas no other tenant had brewed more than three times. In 1390-91 Robert Alynot paid over a lump sum of 6d a year to operate as a general brewer at Cuxham, while half a dozen other villagers still paid for individual

brewings. By the fifteenth century there was a reduction in most villages in the numbers of those brewing for occasional sale and a new class of regular licensed brewers was emerging. Many of these no longer relied on farming for their living, but derived an income, in common with other specialist producers and craftsmen, from supplying their neighbours; they often combined brewing with other activities such as milling, baking or the keeping of an alehouse.

The medieval sources give glimpses of this developing commercialism in ale supply but many questions remain unanswered. Who in the village, for example, were buying in their ale and who were self-sufficient? The balance must have tipped towards purchase from a specialist somewhat earlier in the towns, but details of the move away from home-brewing can be traced only in the fuller Tudor and Stuart records of individual Oxfordshire households.

After the mid-sixteenth century there are surviving wills of local farmers, tradesmen and craftsmen, and inventories detailing their moveable goods at death, valued to enable the estate to be assessed. Some 260 inventories from Oxfordshire have survived from the period 1550-1590 and although none of the individuals is described specifically as a maltster or brewer, there is clear evidence of the wide scale of domestic brewing and, to a lesser extent, malting. Well over a quarter of the households described included specific brewing or malting equipment, usually listed in the kitchen, buttery or bakehouse, although in six of the larger houses a special brewhouse was set aside, called in the local dialect a 'yeiling house'. Two malthouses are mentioned and one maltchamber.

The evidence increases with the greater number of inventories surviving from the seventeenth century. The growth of professional brewing and malting can be observed in the numbers of those described as 'brewer' and 'maltster', but an assessment of the continuing importance of home-brewing in the supply of ale and beer can best be made by detailed study of individual communities. The inventories reveal rising standards of living and wider purchasing horizons for those doing well in an age of growing general prosperity, but even the well-off looked locally for beer supply. Bulky casked beer could not have been economically transported more than 4 or 5 miles.

Banbury in the early seventeenth century was a small country market town of perhaps 300 houses, known chiefly for its cakes, cheese and ale. 'Beverie' had been listed as the town's distinctive product as early as the fourteenth century. Supplies of local malt were plentiful; when, in 1628, a terrible fire destroyed a third of the town, twenty malt kilns were involved in the destruction. Indeed, the fire was believed to have started in a malt kiln, furnishing the Puritan vicar, William Whately, with the opportunity for a fierce sermon on the consequences of over-indulgence. For the period 1621-50 there are 174 surviving wills of Banbury people, mostly with their inventories. Two of these detail the goods of men described as maltsters, but none give their occupation as brewer. Maltsters are recorded in the Banbury parish registers from the late sixteenth century, but the first mention of a brewer is the burial of William Holloway, baker and brewer, in 1716. Forty seven of the inventories, however, refer to the possession of brewing equipment; they are almost entirely of the better-off, with an average value of £76 as against only £20 for those who must have been buying in their beer. Of the two victuallers and two innholders brewing for sale, only one had a brewhouse; the others brewed in kitchen or buttery. Others who could afford to equip a brewhouse included two wealthy yeomen, a widow with large stores of casked beer, one gentleman, a mercer, blacksmith and baker. Farmers were well represented among those who brewed for their own households; most of those who are described as husbandmen or yeomen had brewing vessels and many, especially in the outlying parts of the parish, were malting their own barley.

The close link between baking and brewing in Banbury, still apparent in the nineteenth century, was clearly established by the seventeenth. All five of the bakers whose inventories survive were well supplied with brewing vessels and one was also malting. Of the other town tradesmen, a few of the more prosperous — a smith, a butcher, a tanner, two saddlers, two masons, four glovers, two mercers and two woollendrapers — were brewing their own beer.

Most of the inventories include barrels and beer. Of those who were either buying in supplies or perhaps taking their malt to a neighbour to brew, there are notable groups of labourers, widows, spinsters and servants and the majority of the town's craftsmen, particularly weavers, shoemakers and carpenters.

The prosperous villages of Adderbury, East and West, provide an example of the continuing importance in the countryside of domestic brewing in the 1600s. This was a community largely of farmers, growing a wide range of crops, including barley, on the rich soils of the open fields around the villages. The general level of wealth was greater than in most north Oxfordshire villages at the time. Inventories of 178 Adderbury gentlemen, farmers and craftsmen survive for the period 1600-1700. Of these, 40% have evidence for domestic brewing and 15% for malting, although only one man, (Thomas Penn, who died in 1698) was described as a maltster. As in Banbury, those in Adderbury who could afford brewing equipment were in general the wealthier people in the village. Among the eight with brewhouses were the gentry, the vicar, one of the yeomen farmers and two innholders. John Rousham, one of the innholders, had in 1663 storage capacity in his cellars for over 500 gallons of beer, brewing equipment worth £15 and the only hops mentioned in the village during the century, 40lb. valued at 20s.

Of the farmers, 57% were brewing in kitchen or buttery, as were all the bakers, the millers and the cornchandlers. Those concerned with livestock — the hayward, a grazier and eleven shepherds — did not, however, brew at home; the village craftsmen — masons, smiths, braziers, carpenters and collarmakers — had beer and storage barrels in their houses, but must have bought it locally.

In the 1700s, brewing on a small scale at home became more expensive; high taxes were levied on malt and hops, and fuel, whether wood or imported coal, grew scarce or highly priced. The availability of furze to the poor was reduced with the erosion of common rights in the movement to improve agricultural productivity by enclosure. William Cobbett, writing in the 1820s, maintained that home brewing was common among labourers 40 years before, but by his time it had almost disappeared. The common brewers and public houses enjoyed a virtual monopoly while, in the home, the place of beer had been supplanted by tea, a habit which Cobbett deplored as 'a destroyer of health, an enfeebler of the frame, an

	£	s	d
In the Chamber over the brewhouse			
Two quarter and halfe of mault	3	6	8
Forty pound of hopps	1	0	0
one styll and one lymbicke		10	0
one bushell of salt two old tubbs and other trumpery in the sam chamber		6	8
In the Brewhouse			
One furnace	3	6	8
one meashvate one yeelding vate 3 smaller vates, 3 Coolers and other Copery-ware in the brewhouse	3	6	8
one maultmill	1	0	0
three sackes		4	0
In the Seller			
One pipe, 4 hodggsheads, and 5 halfe hodgsheads	1	0	0
4 hodgheads and halfe of beare	2	0	0
8 flaggons, 3 quart potts, one pint pott and drinkinge glasses	1	0	0

Brewing Equipment, listed in the inventory of John Rowsham, innholder of Adderbury, 1663, with transcript.

engenderer of effeminacy and laziness, a debaucher of youth and a maker of misery for old age'. Cobbett was anxious to revive home brewing amongst tradesmen and labourers, and gave detailed instructions on the processes, but he minimised the problems of providing fuel for a large brew, while tea could be made on the kitchen fire.

Cobbett may have exaggerated the completeness of the move towards tea. An undercurrent of home-brewing was observed by George Herbert in the Banbury of the 1840s, where there were 'brewers who were bakers as well; the two trades were always considered as one. The bakers generally had large back premises, and most of them had a brewery attached so that a person would send his malt to the brewer and tell him how many gallons he required to the bushel of malt. It was then brewed and carried home and turned into his own barrels, but most persons used to have their own plant at home: the baker was then employed at home to brew for them'.

Herbert was looking back from the beginning of this century, by which time home-brewing had virtually died out. It was only in the 1970s, with commercially produced beer kits, that interest in domestic brewing was revived.

Brewing in the Large Household

Brewing was also an important element in providing for the needs of those in the large seigneurial household — extended family, retainers and servants. The making of malt for the lord's brewing was one of the labour services sometimes demanded of tenants during the twelfth and thirteenth centuries; the service was later commuted to a money payment known as *maltpennies* or *maltsilver*. Seigneurial brewing differed from that of the peasant not in the processes but in the scale of the operation and, with the capacity to store large quantities of ale, in the reduced frequency of brewing. In the larger establishments the ale drunk at table might be a year or more old, and a large brew might be undertaken twice a year, in October with the new season's malt and in March to last through the heat of the summer months.

Manor houses and castles often had separate brewhouses to accommodate large scale brewing vessels; these were normally close to or under the same roof as the bakehouse. The brewhouse of Oxford Castle, said in 1255 to have recently collapsed, was replaced by 1267 but was again in disrepair by 1331. An inventory describing all the rooms of *Shirburn Castle* lists a brewhouse there in 1539.

As the great medieval fortified houses finally lost their defensive functions after the Civil War, they continued as the centres of large estates, which could provide malt for the households brewing needs. An inventory of the contents of Broughton Castle in 1731 records a range of service rooms — bakehouse, dairy, washhouse, cellar and brewhouse — which were probably in existence by 1662 but have now disappeared. The Broughton estate also supplied the brewhouse with hops from its own yard in the seventeenth and eighteenth centuries, but this had gone out of use by the time the contents of the Castle and its brewhouse were sold in the 1830s.

Brewhouses were also built as a natural part of the great houses of rising men of new wealth in the seventeenth century. On the death of Walter Jones, rich wool merchant of Witney, in 1663, the equipment of the brewhouse of his mansion at Chastleton gives a clear idea of the large-scale brewing operations of the household. It included the usual coopered wares — coolers and troughs and tubs — a brass kettle, a furnace or boiler and 'three great massinge vates with two hoope' which have more in common with the equipment of the common brewer in large towns than that of the village farmer or tradesman. The brewhouse survives, but all the equipment has gone.

Communal Brewers

Brewing in the Monasteries

Large-scale brewing remained virtually a monopoly of the greater monastic houses in the early Middle Ages. Although many abbeys also had interests in vineyards and orchards and produced their own wine and cider, ale was the normal staple drink. The abbey cellarer usually acted as the master brewer, sometimes with two or three assistants. The records of Abingdon Abbey, for example, contain many references to ale from the late twelfth century onwards. There the cellarer was responsible for providing ale for the monks at dinner and after the service of compline. Jugs of ale were regularly given to various monastic officials in token of their duties.

Malting barley was extensively grown on the abbey's large estates and in 1369 in the pittancer's garden. Abingdon Abbey derived considerable profits from sales of its malt, but the greater part, 383 quarters, was assigned to the cellarer to brew for the abbey's own use. References to *bona cervisia* and *debili cervisia* show different strengths of ale being produced. The original brewhouse and malthouse of Abingdon Abbey almost certainly stood in the south-west corner of the precinct near the mill and the still-extant Checker and Long Gallery.

Bicester Priory also had its own brewhouse; in 1447 the priory's granger accounted for 161 quarters and 4 bushels of malt, used for the brewing of ale for the prior and convent. The canons' own production was insufficient for all their needs, however, and ale was being bought in both for their own consumption and for the entertainment of guests.

Rewley Abbey in 1720, engraved by M. Burghers. The small building in the foreground was then being used as a brewhouse. (Bodleian, Gough Maps 43 fol. 79).

Expenses incurred at the burial of Prior Richard Parentyn in 1434 included '24 quarts of ale bought, besides our own brewing, 4s', while a later account of c 1460-70 records the purchase of 74 gallons of ale bought at 2d a gallon for 8s 6d and a further 93 gallons at 1½d per gallon.

Some indication of individual consumption can be gained from the pensions, normally including food and drink along with lodging, clothing and fuel, which were granted in some monasteries to retired superiors of the house, benefactors and servants. The standard food allowance often stipulated a gallon of good ale a day, and sometimes a second gallon of weak ale. When the austere Archbishop Peckham carried out a visitation of Eynsham Abbey in 1284 he found that the Bishop of Lincoln had provided an unnecessarily liberal pension for the previous abbot, John of Oxford. The archbishop ordered that the former abbot's daily allowance of four loaves and four gallons of ale must be reduced and made to suffice for the monk assigned to him as a companion as well as for himself.

Brewing in the Oxford Colleges

Brewing for a closed community, as practised in the medieval monasteries, had a parallel in the Oxford colleges. Initially the various university institutions in Oxford were supplied by brewers in the town, but subsequently some of the colleges acquired or built their own brewhouses. At least a dozen of the colleges were brewing their own ale at one time or another.

One of the earliest records is from Merton College, where, in 1284, Archbishop Peckham was complaining that the college brewer was being paid the excessive sum of 10 marks a year (a

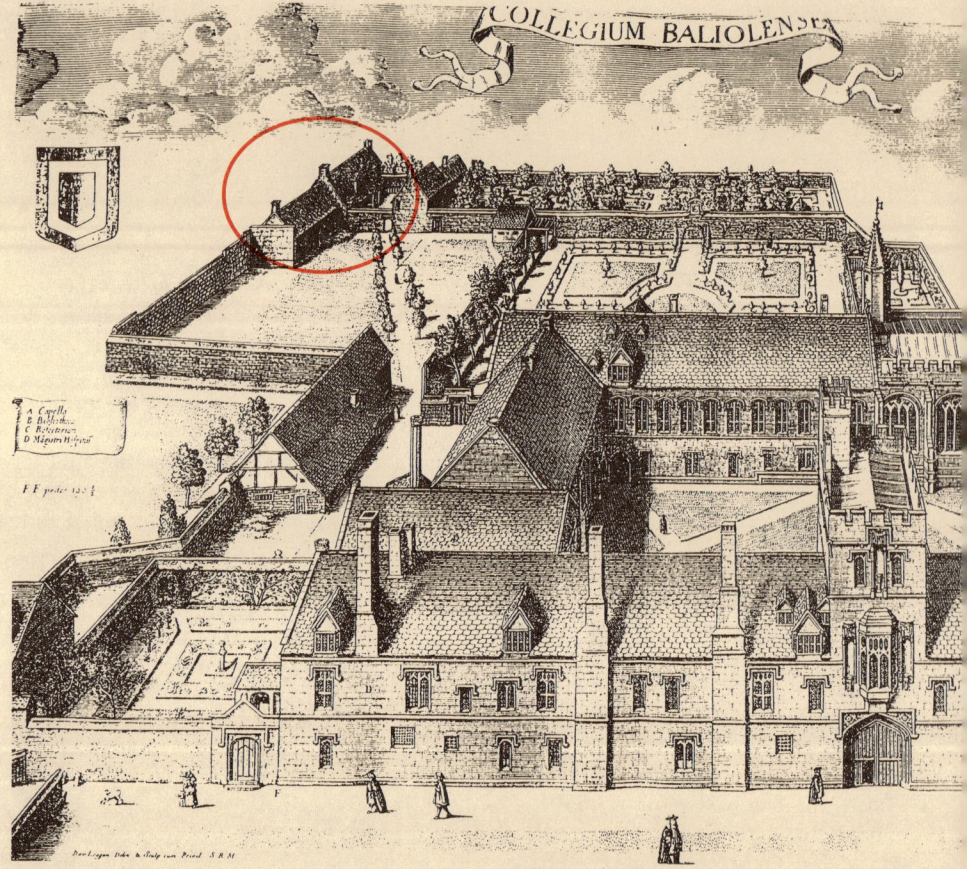

Balliol College, engraved by David Loggan, 1675. The brewhouse (outlined) appears in a plan of 1695.

mark was 6s 8d), though the college's own accounts do not show him receiving more than £1 a year. The office of 'Controller of the Brewery' is first recorded in 1483, and survived up to 1730, when its duties were taken over by the Bursar. The Statutes of Queen's College listed a brewer amongst the college servants at the time of its foundation in 1340-41, and Queen's continued to carry out its own brewing for about 600 years, probably the longest record of continuous brewing on one site or by one institution anywhere in the world. The brewhouse was rebuilt around its medieval core in the sixteenth century, and the timber-framed building still stands today at the west end of the Fellows' Garden. Sadly, brewing ceased there at the outbreak of the Second World War, and the vats became so warped by disuse that resumption was not possible.

The late sixteenth and seventeenth centuries witnessed an expansion in college brewing. A new brewhouse was built at All Souls College in 1594, part of which survives. At Magdalen the first known reference to brewing occurs in an inventory of 1667, when the list of items from the buttery and cellar included 'Three frames for Beare to ly on' and other brewhouse equipment. In 1691 St. John's College purchased a lease of a tenement with a brewhouse and malthouse immediately north of the college and in the same year accounts show that various workmen were putting the premises in order. The freehold of the property was purchased for £467. 5s in 1742. Merton College built a new brewhouse in the Grove in 1691, which lasted until 1827. A brewhouse at Balliol College is recorded for the first time on a map of 1695 and there are records of carpentry and building work here in 1794. A brewhouse built at Brasenose College in 1695-7 cost £300; it survived until 1826.

Several colleges still have their original brewing accounts and inventories of equipment. The Queen's College brewhouse accounts survive for most of the period from 1691 to 1977. The college was brewing both strong and small beer, 'double' and 'middle'. In 1690 purchases of barrels are recorded from coopers as far afield as Blewbury and Thame. On July 27th 1693 the first of a series of inventories of the brewhouse

listed extensive brewing equipment; two years later it was recorded that 'The Hopp basketts and hose (were) much worn, the rest of the utensills in very good order'. Oriel College has brewing books surviving for 1692-1737 and 1850-1867; during the latter period there were never less than 66 barrels a year produced, and in 1866-7 the total rose to 126 barrels. About 4-6 barrels also seem to have been produced every year for the Provost. Corpus Christi's brewhouse account books survive for 1739-99 and 1823-8, with a few years missing, recording the quantities brewed, the costs of malt, hops and occasionally incidental expenses such as coopering, and the amount of excise duty payable. In the first quarter of the academic year 1739-40 four brewings took place, producing 12 barrels of strong beer at £1. 19. 2d each, 17 barrels at £1. 14s and 6 barrels at 6s 6d (presumably weaker small beers). The total brewing expenditure for the whole year was £226. 3s 1d.

Sometimes colleges shared brewing arrangements. On 16th February, 1690, the Warden and Scholars of New College reached agreement with the Provost and Scholars of Queen's College to have occasional use of the brewing vessels and malt-mill belonging to the latter, and in March 1692 the Warden and Fellows of All Souls were granted a similar concession. Brasenose College was permitted to use the St. John's brewhouse in 1692-3; Oriel was similarly allowed to make use of the Merton brewhouse for 12s per brewing. On May 27th 1757 Magdalen supplied Queen's College with two barrels of small beer, presumably to remedy a temporary shortage.

The quality of college ales was often the subject of comment. Archbishop Bancroft, Visitor to All Souls College in 1609, was scandalised at the strength of

the ale produced there: 'It is astonishing the kind of beer which heretofore you have had in your College, and hath been some cause of your decrements; for redress whereof I do strictly charge you by all the authority I have . . . that from henceforth there shall be no other received into your Buttery . . . but either small or middle beer; drink of higher rates being fitter for tippling-houses.' John Aubrey recalled that Dr. Ralph Kettell, President of Trinity College from 1599 to 1643, 'observed that the Houses that had the smallest beer had the most drunkards, for it forced them to go into the towne to comfort their stomachs, Wherefore Dr. Kettell always had in his College excellent beere, not better to be had in Oxon, so that we could not goe to any other place but for the worse, and we had the fewest drunkards of any house in Oxford'. Sometimes the consequences of overindulgence proved fatal. Thomas Hearne records the death, in 1729, of John Whiteside, Keeper of the Ashmolean Museum, from drinking 'a pretty deal of bad small beer at Christchurch'.

College brewing was still thriving in the early 19th century. At Corpus Christi there are detailed accounts for the services of a builder, stonemason, plasterer, plumber and smith in 1823-4 and purchases of new utensils and equipment which suggest a major overhaul of the brewing facilities. The seventeenth century brewhouse at Brasenose was replaced by more modern premises in 1826. Some distinctive special ales were now being produced. Merton College made a strong ale called 'Archdeacon', after E. T. Bigge, college librarian in the early 1840s, who subsequently became Archdeacon of Lindisfarne. 'Chancellor' was a famous triple-brewed Queen's College beer — three barrels brewed in March 1874 cost £21. 12s 0d.

Towards the end of the century, however, decline set in. No brewing is recorded at Magdalen College after 1872, and the brewhouse there had disappeared before 1881. At Merton the brewhouse was pulled down in 1827 and, although brewing continued in the sacristy for some years, the utensils were finally sold in 1878. Oriel's brewhouse was sold in 1883 and soon afterwards removed to make way for new buildings. The Brasenose brewhouse, rebuilt only sixty years before, was demolished to make way for the New Quadrangle in 1886-9. At Corpus Christi the college brewhouse was similarly swept away for new building works in 1927. The Queen's College brewery, the last survivor, succumbed during the Second World War. Pembroke College had long since ceased brewing, but up until the war it had a College Special Beer called Penny Old brewed to its own recipe by a commercial firm. Its last consignment failed to arrive at Oxford railway station in 1939, having apparently been intercepted by the military en route!

Boiling the wort with hops in the copper of the Queen's College brewhouse, 1930s.

Church Ales and Alebedripes

The hard life of the medieval peasant was occasionally relieved by formally-organised drinking sessions at which attendance was compulsory. These might coincide with ceremonies such as marriages (Bride-ales) and funerals (Wake-ales) and regularly occurred when heavy communal works were undertaken. At Cuxham in 1288-9 four quarters of malt were made for the ale drunk at harvest. The lord of the manor used these sessions as another means of raising money. At first they were frowned upon by the Church, but, as it proved impossible to suppress them, the system was adopted for ecclesiastical purposes. The main Church ale was usually held around Whitsuntide, when the churchwardens were expected to go round amongst the parishioners levying specified amounts of wheat and malt. Brewers who attempted to trade when a Church ale was taking place were normally fined by the court. Bequests of malt were sometimes made to the Church. In 1496 Joan Dagenale, widow of Henley-on-Thames, left half a quarter of malt to each of ten different churches, Shiplake, Rotherfield Peppard, Rotherfield Greys, Bix Brand and Pishill in Oxfordshire, Hurley, Wargrave and Remenham in Berkshire and Fawley and Medmenham in Buckinghamshire. In 1520 Magdalen College persuaded the tenants of Headington and Marston to surrender their common rights in the King's Mill Closes in St. Clement's in exchange for a regular payment of a bushel of malt, or 10d and a sheep, or 3s 4d at the time of the church ales. Payment of this due is a recurring feature of the churchwardens' accounts, for example the entry at Marston on April 8th 1561 that 'the busshell of malte that was receyvid of Magdaleyn Colledge was briwyd at Witsontide'. The Whitsun Ale is regularly mentioned, but there was also a church ale at Hocktide in 1546 and an additional 'young men's ale' in 1552. Church ales continued to be a standard way of raising parish funds up to the early seventeenth century.

On some manors ale was regularly provided by manorial lords in exchange for boon-works at times of harvest and haymaking; boon-works where ale was automatically provided were called *alebedripes*. The workers on the Battle Abbey estate at Crowsmarsh were provided at harvest-time with wheaten bread, ale and cheese at noon and with bread, ale, pottage, meat or herrings and cheese at vespers. Ale was also regularly provided in part payment to workmen engaged on all sorts of construction operations. At Henley the expenses of hanging a bell at the Cross included 2d for ale.

The Professionals

During the Middle Ages increasingly successful attempts were made at both national and local level to regulate and control the brewing industry and to exploit it as a means of raising revenue. The documentation surrounding the imposition and collection of taxes and tolls, the drawing-up of regulations and the infringements against them provide some of our major sources of information on the early growth of the trade.

The imposition of a national tax on ale by Henry II in 1188 to help raise money for the third Crusade represents one of the earliest attempts to exploit brewing for revenue purposes on a large scale. At local level there were also tolls and licences known variously as *aletol*, *breugabulum* and *tolsester* which were payable to the lord of the manor whenever brewing took place.

From the early thirteenth century onwards attempts to control prices, monitor quality, and maintain supplies of ale are increasingly evident. Village by-laws and Assizes of Ale enabled the manorial court or the town corporation to amerce all brewers who attempted to sell ale at more than the fixed price and to inflict penalties upon those who offered for sale ale of inferior quality or sold by measures which had not been officially inspected and sealed. In 1267 Henry III fixed the maximum price of ale throughout the kingdom by statute, according to a complicated sliding price scale based upon the seasonal cost of grain. Price fixing took account of two or three different grades or strengths of ale, and also set different rates for boroughs and country villages.

Ale-tasters were appointed to supervise the quality. In 1369 the ale-tasters of Wallingford were themselves amerced for failing to perform their duties to the satisfaction of the court. Anyone brewing for sale had to erect a sign outside his house — traditionally an ivy bunch — to indicate to the ale-taster that his services were required there. In Oxford, in 1254-5, anyone failing to put out a sign was liable to have their ale confiscated and elsewhere fines were frequent. In 1384 Elias Preston of Wallingford was fined not only for refusing to put up a sign outside his house but also for refusing to sell ale out of his house. Brewers were compelled to produce at least a specified minimum quantity for sale even when the price of malt made the operation unprofitable, otherwise supplies literally dried up.

Regulations were also introduced to prevent the contamination of water habitually used by brewers and to dissuade the brewers themselves from using contaminated water. This was a particular problem in the towns. In 1293 brewers in Oxford were forbidden to use the 'corrupt water' of the Trill Mill Stream.

From the presentment of offences against the Assizes of Ale it is evident that it was normally more profitable to infringe the regulations and pay the fines rather than not to brew at all. Many of the offenders were perfectly respectable people who held responsible positions: two of the offenders in Wallingford in 1369 were aldermen of the town. The routine of regular presentments and amercements seems to have become simply a form of licensing.

The Medieval Town Brewer

Brewers start appearing in town records around the beginning of the thirteenth century. The burghmote roll of Wallingford for 1233, which lists several women 'amerced for ale' is one of the earliest records of the enforcement of the assizes of ale. While most people were initially brewing for occasional sale while pursuing other occupations, the rise of the specialist professional brewer began rather earlier in the towns than in the countryside. One Ralph the Brewer, who was acquiring land in Oxford from St. Frideswide's Priory in 1240, was already then a man of some prominence in the town. Even so, most Oxford burgesses were still engaged in some brewing in the early fourteenth century, though the numbers of occasional brewers were in decline.

Two disruptions which occurred in the middle of the fourteenth century resulted in a restructuring of Oxford's brewing industry. Many brewers died in the Black Death. Between October 1348 and October 1349 the number of amercements for breaches of the assize of ale fell from 221 to 161 individuals, and the low coincidence of names — only 18% — suggests that many of the latter were new immigrants or people who had just taken up the trade. The other important event was the St. Scholastica's Day Riot of February 10th, 1355, which began with an affray in the Swindlestock Tavern on Carfax and resulted in the plundering of the University halls and colleges by the townspeople. In the judgement which followed, the powers of the University were further extended over the City. The supervision of the assize of ale and the profits arising from it, which had been divided jointly between the City's Mayor and the University's Chancellor, now came under sole control of the Chancellor.

The University's control of the assize of ale had far-reaching effects and contributed greatly to the rising importance of brewers in Oxford in the

Fifteenth century brewhouse, from a German woodcut. Even in commercial breweries, coopered wooden vessels such as these remained in use for another 400 years.

later Middle Ages. Initially a rota system was organised which forbade some citizens from brewing for sale while others were brewing and insisted that brewers due to brew on stated days did so, regardless of the price of malt or their own convenience. The effect of this was to reduce the number of citizens who found occasional brewing a profitable sideline and to concentrate production in the hands of a smaller number of increasingly prosperous specialists. The Poll Tax of 1381 listed 32 brewers in the City, plus 54 servants attached to their households who were often apprentices of the trade; there were also ten innkeepers, seven tapsters and three taverners. There were probably also still quite a number of part-time brewers and beer retailers who escape notice because they are recorded under their main occupation. The prosperity of the brewers is underlined by the fact that many of them were assesed for high amounts, from 6s 8d up to 13s 4d, compared with the average payment of 1s.

Brewers and taverners rising up the social scale came to figure more prominently amongst the town bailiffs after 1350, and over the next 150 years no less than ten brewers, vintners and taverners went on to serve as Mayors of Oxford. One of these was John Sprunt, who probably came originally from Essex. By about 1400 he had acquired half a dozen properties in various parts of the city. In a house in Queen Street called *'domus Durham'* which backed onto Shoe Lane, we find that Sprunt brewed ale and was fined for throwing out dirty water and ashes into Shoe Lane. This property still contained a brewhouse in 1535 when it was being leased out by All Souls College. Another of Sprunt's former properties on the High Street contained a brewhouse when All Souls College leased it out in 1467. John Sprunt died in 1419, and his will lists taverner's equipment, including various wood, lead and brass vessels.

By the end of the fourteenth century, as brewing was becoming more concentrated in the towns, the ouput of the professional town brewers began to rival that of the monasteries. The University continued to exert its control over brewing in Oxford. In 1434 the University's Commissary, Christopher Knollys, summoned the City's brewers to St. Mary's Church to complain of malpractices which had appeared and to reorganise and enforce the rota; they were to supply sufficient malt for brewing and see to it that two or three brewers sent out their ale for public sale two or three times a week; the name of each brewer and the dates when he was to brew were set down. In 1500-1 the University experimented with a longer rota under pressure to favour the poorer brewers, but a shortage of ale resulted.

The control of the quality was strictly enforced. In 1449 nine Oxford brewers were accused of brewing weak and unwholesome ale which was not properly prepared and not worth the price being charged. They were made to swear that in future they would brew in a wholesome manner, that they would continue to heat the water over the fire so long as it emitted froth and would then skim the froth off, and that after skimming they would allow the new ale to stand long enough for its dregs to settle before sending it out. Richard Benet in particular had to undertake not to send any of his ale out to any hall or college until it had stood for at least twelve hours.

The Lay Subsidy returns of 1524 show that there were then 15 full-time and 11 part-time brewers in Oxford. The specialist brewers stand out from the rest

of the City's tradesmen and craftsmen, accounting for about twenty per cent of its entire assessed wealth. Under the administration of the University the brewers had begun to develop a corporate guild organisation during the fifteenth century, and the guild attempted to develop a monopoly in the City. In 1525 it was ordained that there should be sixteen brewers and no others practising in Oxford; but this was resisted by the University Commissary in 1530, who complained that 'Mychaell Hethe and other of the brewers of Oxford, will let no man entre unto the crafte of bruers, unlese all or the more parte of the said crafte will agree thereunto'. The restrictions appear to have been relaxed and during the later sixteenth century the brewers no longer had quite the same domination of the town that they had enjoyed earlier.

Records of brewing in the small market towns are more spasmodic, but one gets the same impression of its rising prominence at the end of the Middle Ages. In the middle of the fifteenth century the manorial records of Bicester record one massive purchase of 132½ gallons of ale from John Spinan, Alice Bedale and a few other brewers in the town, which cost 4s 10d. Henry VI's Charter to Woodstock in 1453 granted the Mayor and Commonalty the right to have the assize of ale when it should become necessary, and there are records of price fixing and the appointment of ale-tasters up to 1758. Robert Brun was fined 40s in 1629 for refusing to take on the office of ale-taster when his turn came. The Witney court drew up a complex series of regulations concerning the brewing and selling of ale in 1549 and in 1555 the assize of ale was entrusted to the mayor and burgesses of the town by its Charter.

Memorial brass of John Sprunt, brewer, (died 1419) in the church of St. Peter-le-Bailey, Oxford.

13

Hops affected both the flavour and the preservative qualities of the beer, allowing storage over a longer period and wider distribution. This made possible a new kind of brewer who sold his wares with reliability to a range of customers and alehouses, for common consumption. These Common Brewers, producing on a far larger scale than their predecessors, appeared in London in the later 1500s and strengthened their position during the next hundred years. Their numbers rose from 26 in 1578-85 to 194 by 1699, when collectively they were producing nearly 130 times more than the brewing publicans.

In Oxfordshire the pattern was repeated on a smaller scale. Already by the end of the sixteenth century there are indications that Henley was beginning its long association with brewing. In 1587 Evans Arderne 'was authorised and allowed to be beerebrewer, and to brew good and holesome drink for man's bodye'. In 1608 orders were issued in the town establishing the price of beer. Barrels of the best beer were to be sold at 8s, with small beer at 5s.

In Oxford in the seventeenth century, brewers and maltsters were wealthy men of position. Oliver Smyth, a brewer, was mayor in 1619, 1624 and 1631; his son

The Common Brewer

A Brewhouse

A common brewer's establishment of the eighteenth century. Note the mash-vat (D), the man pumping the wort up into the copper of the coal-fired furnace (A), the louvres for controlling temperature, and the racking of the beer into casks (inset). From the Universal Magazine, 1747.

14

Thomas, who followed him as brewer, was elected mayor in 1638 and 1643 and another son, John, a maltster, succeeded as mayor in 1639. Other brewers and maltsters regularly served as bailiffs and mayors throughout the century. During all this time the University continued to exercise its authority over the brewers, attempting to ensure supplies of an acceptable standard. Vice-Chancellor Bathurst issued a notice in June 1676, claiming that 'it hath been observed yt the Common Brewers of this place, consulting more yr own private gain than the health and benefit of others, have not of late years made ye beer and ale of equall goodness with that of former times' and ordering that they 'take particular care, yt the said sorts of Beer and Ale . . . be made good and wholesome and agreeable to the assize.' In 1701 Vice-Chancellor Roger Mander ordered 'that no public Ale Brewers nor Beer Brewers within the precincts of this University, presume to sell their double Beer or Ale for more than ten shillings the barrell (besides the duty of Excise)'.

In the century and a half from 1700 the county's breweries grew in numbers and in size; brewing became one of the most important local industries, and the brewery became one of the most conspicuous industrial buildings in all the towns and in many of the villages. The most important factor in this growth was the general increase in population, especially in the nineteenth century. At the same time a decline in domestic and alehouse brewing meant better sales for the common brewer.

In Oxford, the 1700s saw the emergence of the geat brewing families, all closely related — the Halls, Treachers, Morrells and Tawneys — who came to dominate the trade. There were, in addition, numerous smaller concerns and publican brewers working behind their retail premises. Their businesses, however, were generally short-lived, and the pages of Jackson's Oxford Journal regularly carry notices for the lease or sale of brewing premises following the death of their previous occupants.

These common breweries were concentrated in the town centre, with a large number in St. Aldates and Brewers Lane, Queen Street and Cornmarket, and others in St. Giles' and St. Thomas's, where many maltsters were also located. The more long-lasting of these smaller breweries were those of Henry Drought and Charles Moore, both in the St. Aldates/Brewers Lane area from the 1750s to the 1780s, and both passing their breweries on to sons.

Before then, however, what were to become Oxford's two great breweries had become established. The Swan's Nest Brewery was already in existence by 1718 and, surviving through the century, had passed into the ownership of Sir John Treacher by 1780; he in turn sold it to William Hall in 1795. Even older as a brewing location was that which eventually became Morrell's brewery site in St. Thomas's; a 'brewhouse and garden' are referred to in a lease of 1597, though there is no further mention of brewing there until 1718. By 1745 the lease was held by Richard Tawney, brewer, and it remained in the hands of the Tawney family until 1803, when it passed to Mark and James Morrell.
(continued on page 22)

Advertisement for the sale of the equipment of a brewery, Jackson's Oxford Journal, 1735.

Billhead of William Barker, brewing victualler at the Three Tuns, Horsefair, Banbury, mid-eighteenth century.

Barley reaping,
woodcut by Thomas Bewick.

Barley into Malt: early malting processes

In the south of England barley has always been the main cereal used for malting, though there are medieval references to the use of dredge — barley and oats sown together — and occasionally wheat, oats and even beans might be added to the malt.

The purpose of malting was to make soluble the starches and proteins contained in the hard grain. Germination was induced by steeping it in water until it was swollen and soft and then draining and spreading it to warm up and absorb oxygen. As soon as the grain sprouted, its growth was stopped by drying and sometimes by roasting in a kiln. This gave the malt its biscuit-like flavour and texture.

During the early Middle Ages malting was the universal means of using up surplus barley and other cereals. The amount of malt produced might vary considerably from year to year, depending on the harvest. The manorial accounts of Cuxham, for example, show that between 1276 and 1279 a considerable proportion of the barley and dredge was grown primarily for sale after malting. In 1288-9 the sale of the grain itself achieved great prominence, only enough malt being made for the manor's own needs. Very little malt was sold during the ensuing decade, but the production of malt for sale recommenced in 1299-1300 and from then until the Black Death in the mid-fourteenth century up to 26 quarters were made annually. There are also occasional references at Cuxham to the malting of small quantities of wheat.

Also at Cuxham there is an interesting reference to the reconstruction, in 1301-2, of a detached oven within the manorial precinct, and to the replacement of this oven with a new one in 1336-7. Its principal purpose seems to have been to generate the gentle heat needed for malting. There were frequent purchases of hurdles and rough cloth (heyre) for it, upon which the grain would have been spread to dry; in 1278-9 a purchase of heyre for 3s was stated specifically to be for drying malt.

On many manors the tenants were obliged to grind their malt at the lord's mill. The mill at Cottisford in 1292 produced 30s from sales of malt and maslin (a mixture of wheat and rye). A description of Wallingford Castle in 1300 lists two malting mills within its precincts. On the estate of the Knights Templars at Sibford Gower in 1311, although no barley was grown, malt was still included amongst the tolls of the mill. The obligation to use the lord's mill for malting was always difficult to enforce and often lapsed later in the Middle Ages, but in 1568 all Oxford brewers were still bound to have their grinding done at the Castle Mill; as late as 1594 it was recorded that most of the inhabitants of Thame had been accustomed to using the lord's malt mill at Old Thame.

The basic malting process remained unchanged for centuries and a description by Gervase Markham at the beginning of the seventeenth century is probably a reasonable guide to medieval practice:

'They take a good quality of barley and put it into a Cesterne or vat and so steepe it in water the space of 3 nights, then drain it from the water and let it drop a day, then lay it on a faire floore in a great thick heap or centre, and let it so lie 3 nights more, in which space it will sprout at one end (for it must not sprout at both): then they spread it very thin all over the flower, and either with a shovell or the hand it must be turned and tossed twice or thrice a day, for the space of 14 days more (for to make perfect Malte it must have full 3 weeks Vat and Floor), then they drie it upon the Kilne with a gentle fire, of sweete straw, (for any other fuell yields too strong a smoake and gives the Malt an ill taste) after the

Malt is dried cooled, rubbed cleane skreened and winnowed, then it is sent to the Mill and ground according to the proportion of the Brewing.'

The basic equipment was simple — a cistern to steep the barley, an area of floor for growing and some method of drying the barley, commonly a coarse cloth made of horsehair for spreading on a wooden frame over the fire. The cistern is usually referred to as a *yeoting* vat (from yote, to soak). The hair cloths are sometimes called oast or kiln hairs. Edward Kempsale of Bampton had 'one yottying fat' in 1559. John Ives of Great Milton, husbandman, had one in 1562, together with four quarters of malt, and brewing and baking equipment. Elizabeth Howes of Cropredy, widow, in 1577 had a 'yoitinge fatte' and a 'heare for to drye malt, 4 sackes, 2 malt seves, 2 wynoing seves and a busshel', as well as brewing utensils. Richard Day of Wheatley in 1585 actually had a malthouse containing 'an old yotinge Fatte, other tubes and cooperie Ware and half a Querne'.

Of the 259 Oxfordshire inventories published for the period 1550-1590, mostly of craftsmen and farmers, 32 (12½%) contain references to malting equipment. Although not as high a proportion as those engaged in domestic brewing, it still suggests that malting was an important occupation in a considerable number of households. From Banbury inventories we know that a quarter of malt was valued at £1 3s in 1627 and £2 in 1631. In the same year six quarters of 'green malt upon the floors' were worth £6. By this time some of those engaged in malting were beginning to see the commercial sense of becoming full time professionals and, as their numbers grew and production increased, that of the domestic operator declined.

Good and holesome drynke: early brewing processes

Evidence for early brewing, as for malting, comes in the main from two sources — inventories of household equipment, made after death for probate purposes, and the descriptions of contemporaries: archaeological evidence or surviving equipment are almost non-existent. There is one early find, however; in 1967 a large thirteenth century pottery vessel was discovered at Churchill and interpreted as a cistern used in the brewing or, more probably, storage of ale. A bung-hole at the base is so placed as to allow liquor to be drawn off without disturbing the sediment; its capacity is about sixteen gallons.

With the exception of a vessel, whether pottery or metal, for heating over the fire, all other brewing vessels in the Middle Ages were no doubt of coopered wooden construction,

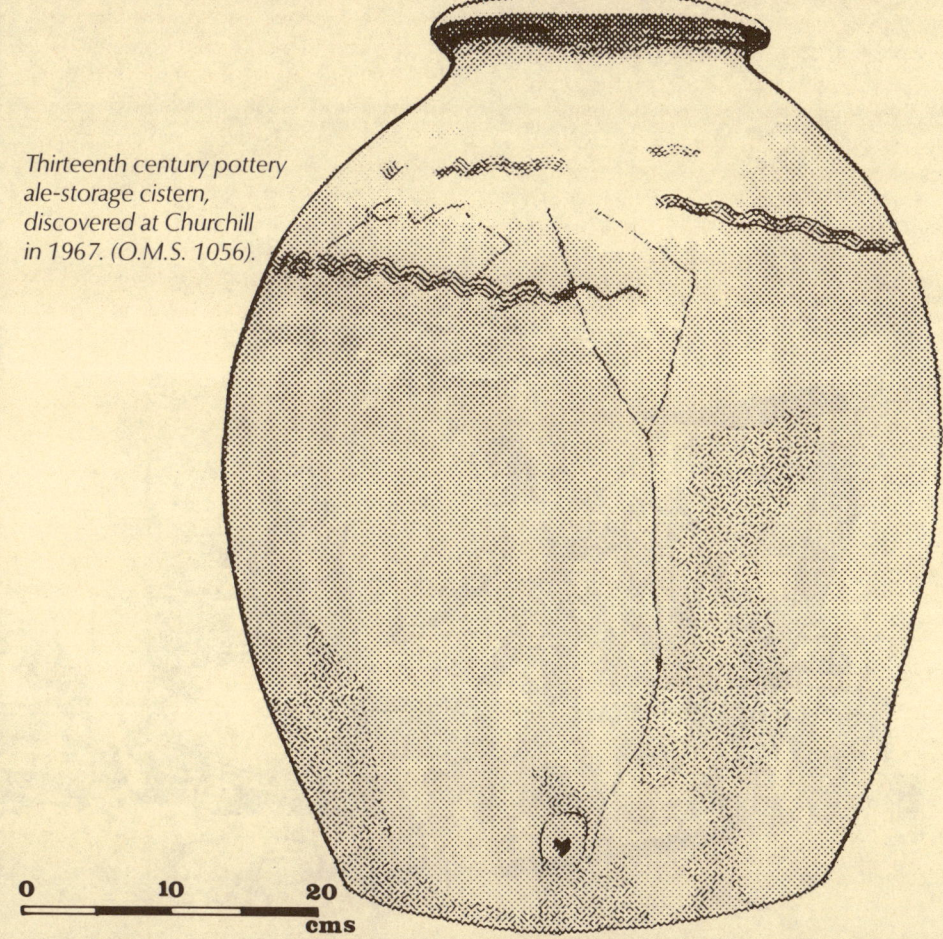

Thirteenth century pottery ale-storage cistern, discovered at Churchill in 1967. (O.M.S. 1056).

0   10   20
cms

Some of the equipment noted in later household inventories probably reflects medieval practice fairly faithfully, as do later descriptions; that of Gervase Markham at the beginning of the seventeenth century summarises the basic processes, although he is speaking of hopped beer rather than medieval ale:

'After the Malt is ground they put it into a mashvat and the liquor in the Lead being ready to boyle, put it to the malt and mash altogether. Let it stand an howre. Then drain the liquor from the Malt and put it in the lead againe, and ad to it for every quarte of Malt a 1½lbs of hops and boyle over for the space of an howre. Then clense the liquor from the hops through a straight sive into the Cooler . . . then put in your barme (i.e. yeast) and after they have wrought, then heate them together and doe this so: divers times together, then tunne your Beere into Hoggsheads, let it purdge well, and after closse them up. This Beere may be drunke at a fortnight's age and is of long lasting.'

The first step was to crush the malt and, by the sixteenth century, the malt mill was a fairly common item of equipment; William Howarth, baker of Kidlington, had a 'moltt querne' worth 13s 4d in 1565, and they remained valuable items — one in Banbury was worth £1 13s 4d in 1631. They were probably paired hand-turned stones set in a wooden frame; an inventory of 1577 refers to 'an old frame for a myle'. After crushing and collecting (a Witney inventory of 1584 includes 'a mallte querne with a thing to sett under hym') the grist would be sieved before putting with the hot water in the mash vat. There is a distinction apparent in the inventories between vessels called *vats*, which were of wood (coopered and often appearing under the 'coperye wares') and *leads* in which the liquor was heated. Some of these do seem to have been of lead, though brass and copper probably became more common. The 'leads' or 'kettles' must have been portable

cauldrons, set over a fire, though there are also references to 'furnaces'. Mrs Catherine Doylye, widow of Merton in 1585, had 'a newe furnesse' valued at £1, the high value being perhaps explained by later mentions of brass and copper furnaces, though Richard Kimble, Banbury yeoman in 1625, had one of lead. Another Banbury yeoman, Isaac Showell, had two in 1625, both of copper, a large one worth £8 and a smaller one at £4 10s. This must be the item of equipment later known simply as a copper, and it may already at this early date have been a fixed piece of equipment, set over a fire grate. Some apparently had covers; one in Banbury in 1639 had 'a furnace door'. Wherever heated, the water would have to be transferred to the mash-vat in the 'payles' which appear regularly with other brewing equipment. The wooden mashvats might be set on stands — that of Thomas Foster, mercer of Banbury in 1621, had a 'still or standard' possibly for ease of drawing off the sweet wort into

Domestic brewing processes, illustrate W. H. Pyne for his 'Microcosm', 1808: grinding the malt, mashing, stoking the furnace, fermenting and racking the be

the 'wortpan' after mashing. Wortpans were sometimes specified as being of brass: 'fyve brasen woortpannes' were valued at £2 in 1583. The next stage, boiling with hops, was carried out in the lead or kettle again, or in the furnace. Hops were occasionally listed in later sixteenth century inventories. Mrs Doylye of Merton had a malt chamber containing, among other things, 'hoppes with the bagge' and Thomas Taylor of Witney in 1583 had 'an olde Coarse Canvas Bagge with hopps in hym' valued at 2s 6d. After boiling the wort had to be cooled in vessels described variously as coolers, cooling kivers, or troughs, which seem always to have been of wood. When at the right temperature it was transferred in pails to the fermenting vat, called the 'Bruyinge fatte' (1587) or more usually 'yeiling' vat; this, again, seems to have been of wood. The yeast was added and as it multiplied, the surplus might be skimmed off with an implement called a skip.

When fermentation was complete, and the brew had cooled, it was ready for transferring into casks for storage. Many inventories refer to 'barrells' and some to the 'styles' or standards on which they were set. Mrs Doylye had '11 barrells and beare vessels' in the buttery.

Some inventory references differentiate between ale and beer. In Banbury, a 'barrell of ale' was valued at 2s 4d in 1631, a hogshead at 7s 6d in 1635. Beer was valued more highly by the apprisers — a hogshead at 15s in 1627, 10s in 1630, £1 in 1638. Randolph Symes, baker in 1622, had three hogsheads of beer in the cellar, valued at £3, with eight empty vessels at £1 6s 8d.

Brewing was a seasonal activity, as it was even with the commercial brewers well into the nineteenth century. Since fermentation was unpredictable in the warmer months, the March brewing was traditionally the time for making a strong brew to see the household through the summer. In October, brewing was recommended with fresh supplies of malt. Gervase Markham described how 'if it be ordinary household beere, then they draw of every quarte of Malt, 3 hoggsheads of Beere. But if it be for extraordinary strong *March* beere, then to every hoggshead you shall allow one quarte of Maulte, a peck of Pease, half a pecke of Wheate and half a peck of Oats'.

With the end of the period during which inventories were made, we lose sight of the details of domestic brewing, but it must have remained little altered through the years of decline to the 1820s, when William Cobbett was arguing fervently for its revival amongst the labouring classes. His detailed description in *'Cottage Economy'* could serve as a set of instructions for today's home brewer.

Wooden malt shovel and mash tun rowser of the type illustrated by Pyne, common items of equipment in both domestic and professional malting and brewing. (O.M.S. 80.96.987 and 79.167.4).

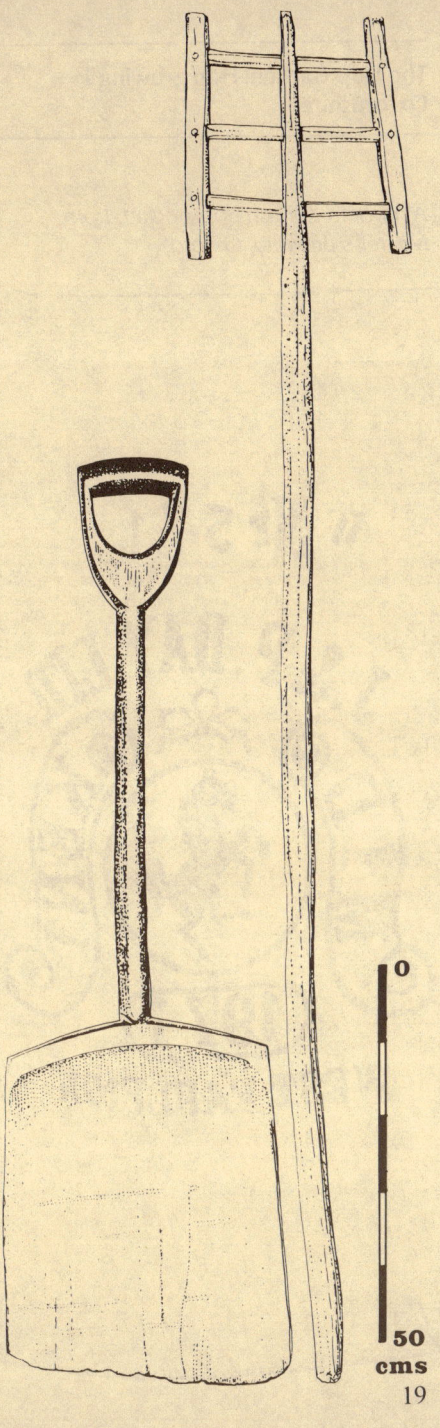

0

50 cms

The Hop Garden: Hop growing in Oxfordshire

A modern Kentish hop-pocket, from Morrell's Brewery, Oxford.

The female flowers of the hop plant contain a resin which has flavouring and preservative properties, and also tannin, which acts as a clarifying agent. Wild hops may have been used amongst many other gruit herbs from an early date; there are some indications that hops were already being cultivated near Paris in the eighth century, and that German brewers were using hops in the ninth century. The plant remains found in an excavated Saxon boat at Graveney in Essex indicate that wild hops were being collected in England by about 1000 AD, though there is no evidence for their use again before the later Middle Ages. References to the use of hops in Oxfordshire first appear in probate inventories in the second half of the sixteenth century, though the earlier records are ambiguous, since the term oast originally applied to malt as well as hop kilns. The possessions of John Ives, husbandman of Great Milton, included, at the time of his death in 1562, an 'olde ost here'. This was a horsehair cloth or mat upon which the hops were spread in a layer 6 inches deep, laid over a platform of battens set at the throat of a chimney above a charcoal or anthracite brazier for drying. They had to be turned every few hours, and the draught and fire needed to be carefully regulated. Similar entries appear in the inventories of William Horskins, husbandman, of Shirburn in 1581 ('an hoste heire'), Thomas Taylor of Witney, yeoman, in 1583 ('parte of a heare cloth for a nost') William Cobb of Dorchester in 1584 ('a her for a nost') and Margaret Penny of Benson in 1588 ('an ostheare'). There is also some archaeological evidence: sixteenth century deposits from the privy of the provost of Oriel College, Oxford, included pollen of the *Cannabiaceae* family, which seems to be more likely from hops used in brewing than from

hemp, the other British representative of that family.

Perhaps the first unambiguous indication that hops were being grown locally appears in the inventory of a Witney baker, Nicholas Hill, in 1589-90; his estate included 'At the Rivers syde, the poles at the hoppe yarde'. Another early local reference to cultivation occurs in the farm accounts of Robert Loder at Harwell in 1613-1620, though it is difficult to assess their annual value since they are always lumped together with the valuation of the farm's walnuts. The further spread of small domestic hopyards during the seventeenth century can be traced from field names on estate maps, terriers and similar documents: a 'Hopyard' appears at Wallingford in 1632, 'The Hop Yard' at Steventon in 1654 and 'Hopyard Close Pasture' at Coleshill in 1666. In these early hopyards the stocks were planted in mounds, two or three to a mound, 5 or 8 feet apart, and trained up poles 13 to 16 feet long.

Although the hop was an unpredictable plant, many Oxfordshire farmers in the eighteenth and nineteenth centuries cultivated a few acres. Over forty field-names have been traced which indicate former hopyards and hopfields. They occur all over Oxfordshire, with the exception of the higher parts of the Chilterns and the country between Wychwood and the Upper Thames. Later hopyards were larger with a different style of cultivation, the plants set in ridged rows with more elaborate systems of poling and wiring. Arthur Young in 1813 describes the five-acre hop plantation which Sir Christopher Willoughby had been cultivating at Marsh Baldon over the last 27 years; on sandy loam soil, it produced anything from no crop at all in some years up to 18cwt per acre; in others the hops might sell from 3

guineas to 14 guineas per hundredweight.

Hop cultivation in Oxfordshire had already begun to decline in the eighteenth century as large-scale commercial hop growers in Kent, Herefordshire and Worcestershire began to capture the market which they retain today. By the end of the century very few hops were grown in Oxfordshire. Morlands of Abingdon, however, still acquire a proportion of their hops from their farm at Kingston Bagpuize. There is one farm hopkiln or oasthouse remaining at East Hagbourne, together with the foundations of two others there, but this distinctive type of farm building never became a common feature of the Oxfordshire landscape.

Hop flowers, and a page from Reynolde Scot's 'A Perfite Platforme of a Hoppe Garden', 1574, showing the training of the plants up poles set on a mound.

Then you may with the forked ende, thrust vp, or throwe off, all such stalkes as remayne vpon cche Hoppe Poale, and carie them to the floore prepared for that purpose.

The best and readyest way to take the Hoppes from the Poales.

For the better doing hereof, it is very necessarie that your Poales be streyght without scrags or knobbes.

In any wise cut no more stalks than you shall cary away within one houre or two at the most, for if in the meane time the Sunne shyne hote, or if it happen to rayne, the Hoppes (remayning cut in that sorte) will be much impayred thereby.

Let all such as helpe you, stande rounde about the floore, and suffer them not to pyngle in picking one by one, but let them speedily strype them into Baskets prepared ready therefore.

It is not hurtfull greatly though the smaller leaues be mingled with the Hoppes.

Remem=

(continued from page 15)

In the rest of the county things were very much the same, with a succession of small one-man brewery concerns which came and went, but also the establishment of soundly based common breweries which remained in one family, expanded and survived. Most of them began as modest enterprises, set up by maltsters or brewing victuallers before concentrating on brewing alone — Morland's of West Ilsley and later Abingdon (1711); Brakspear's of Henley, (1779, building on the earlier Brooks's and Hayward's brewery); Wells of Wallingford (1720); Haywards of Watlington (late eighteenth century) and Hitchman's of Chipping Norton (1796). Their success was due to a number of factors — an amount of good luck, good business sense, good brewing practice, capital to invest in necessary plant, and, in some cases, the acquisition of tied houses to ensure sales. Competition in South Oxfordshire after 1785 was intense, with Brakspear's, Haywards, Wells and Simonds of Reading seeking control of houses in the area, either through ownership or through financial control of the publicans. Here, developments were actually ahead of those in London.

Other breweries sprang up in the first half of the nineteenth century. Demand for beer was unprecedented, despite the growth of temperance movements, from both urban and rural workers, and their families. Beer, which used English malt and hops, was promoted as infinitely preferable to gin. The Beerhouse Act, 1830, abolished the duty on beer and encouraged an increase in the number of outlets by allowing any householder with two guineas to spare to sell beer and cider at his house. Malt and hops were still taxed, discouraging home brewing.

22

Thomas Hunt's brewery in Banbury was established in the 1830s, Clinch's at Witney and John Harris's at Hook Norton in the 1840s. Clinch's were a banking family who moved into brewing, Thomas Hunt and John Harris both started as maltsters. These were well known businesses which survived into recent times, but there were many more, large and small, whose names appear in the Trade Directories, but who vanished long ago: Hilliard's of Wallingford, opened 1830; Byles' Brewery, Henley, established 1823; Cheer's of Abingdon, 1830s; Austins, in the early 1800s the biggest brewery in Banbury; Wyatts, also of Banbury, built between 1837 and 1840; Shillingfords Brewery, Bicester, established in 1846; the Shutford Brewery founded by Mr George Cross in 1840 and still operating in 1905; Walter's brewery in Buckland. In Oxford there were the St. Clement's Brewery, a sizeable concern when sold in 1830, and the St. Giles' Brewery, set up at about the same time. One very particular Oxford brewery was that at the Radcliffe Infirmary, reminiscent of the college or monastic breweries of the Middle Ages. The brewhouse here operated from 1770 until 1853, brewing once a month, with small beer for the patients, ale for the nurses and other staff. Any strong beer not fit for drinking might be used for poultices. After 1853, other Oxford breweries supplied the Infirmary with the patients' daily ration of 1½ pints a day.

Morland's tower brewery at Abingdon, designed by Joseph Wood of Birmingham, built 1911-12 and still in use today.

The Beer Factory

The mid 1800s were the high point of brewing prosperity, and breweries were numerous. By 1860 every Oxfordshire town had at least one, and a number had many more, with 14 in Oxford, 10 in Banbury, 7 in Bicester, 5 in Abingdon, 4 in Deddington, 3 in Witney and Wantage, 2 in Eynsham, Wallingford, Watlington and Henley; single breweries elsewhere brought the total for the area to over seventy.

Fifty years later this number had dwindled to eighteen, and some of these were to vanish very soon afterwards. The tremendous contraction reflects a national trend — of 50,000 breweries in the United Kingdom in 1840 barely 3,000 were left by 1900. There was no matching reduction in beer production, however; brewing simply became concentrated in the hands of fewer and larger concerns, growing at the expense of their rivals. The later eighteenth century and early nineteenth century had seen a growth in

the scale and complexity of brewing, especially in London and Burton, with a constant move towards greater mechanization. Although much of brewing remained labour intensive (especially malting, bottling, coopering and distribution) new industrial techniques, particularly steam power, were available for the enterprising brewer; the common brewhouse was becoming the great industrial brewery.

In Oxfordshire, this expansion and mechanisation only came when the scale of production merited it, around the middle years of the nineteenth century. Hunt, Edmunds of Banbury, starting from small beginnings, became very much an industrial Victorian brewery in these years. Thomas and John Hunt of the Unicorn Inn, Banbury, bought a small malthouse in Bridge Street in 1835, turned to brewing and gradually expanded as Austin's, the

biggest Banbury brewery, declined. After building a new brewhouse in 1848, Thomas Hunt took into partnership William Edmunds who brought capital and brewing expertise to the business. A valuation of 1858 shows what modern plant was being invested in — large cast iron vessels, a Capital Refrigerator, a malt-dressing machine and a Tizard's Patent Mashing Machine with revolving spargers. Development of the brewery was completed in 1866 with the construction of the great malthouse.

Hunt, Edmunds grew large by piecemeal development, and most local breweries responded to modernisation by building onto or adapting older buildings; William Brakspear, for instance, who had

The consolidation of Oxfordshire's breweries between 1860 and 1910. Each barrel symbol represents one independent commercial brewing enterprise.

installed a refrigerator in 1836, built a new boiler house in 1857, and by 1865 a steam engine was providing all the power for milling and pumping; around this time too, an artesian well was sunk. His sons built a new coopers shop in 1886 and a new brewhouse in 1892.

Others, however, completely replaced their old premises with a new and distinctive type of building — the tower brewery. Phillips in Oxford, Townsends and Morlands in Abingdon and the Hook Norton Brewery, for example, were building towers in the years between 1870 and 1912. They were a source of great pride to the firms who built them and, as prominent landmarks, were used extensively in their advertising.

Such developments were plainly impossible without considerable capital resources, and another feature of the later nineteenth century was the converting of flourishing family brewing concerns into limited companies in order to acquire share capital. Those able to raise finance, in this or other ways, were able to expand into modern plant and hope to prosper. Those who could not, or were unable to sustain expansion, were weakened and ripe for take-over by their more successful competitors. The purpose of take-overs was seldom to gain more brewing capacity; it was normal to close down a brewery once aquired, perhaps turning it into a store or distribution centre.

It was this process which reduced Oxfordshire's breweries so drastically. The general trend of the late nineteenth century is complicated, however, by the setting up of a handful of new firms, plainly attracted by the profitability of brewing. Few lasted any length of time. In Abingdon a number of new brewery companies opened up, but all had fallen to Morlands by 1900. In Oxford, Weaving's Eagle Steam Brewery was

taken over by Halls in 1897; the Walton Brewery in Jericho and Phillips' Tower Brewery in Park End Street (despite acquiring the Buckland brewery and one in Faringdon) failed to see out the century. Goodwins at Eynsham, set up in the early 1850s, went to Halls in 1898; the other Eynsham brewers, Gibbons, lasted only from the 1860s to the 1890s. The Sun Brewery in Banbury, in existence by 1863, was taken over by Hunt, Edmunds in 1884.

Some of the new establishments lasted a little longer; the small Ives Brothers Brewery in Market Street, Henley, survived from the early 1880s until the First World War; Gundry's at Goring, set up about the same time, lasted until bought by Brakspear's during the Second War; Garne's of Burford did not stop brewing until 1969. But generally those firms which managed to survive into the twentieth century were all founded before 1850, and were mostly the ones engaged in the take-overs.

In Oxford, as we have seen, Halls were particularly active, after becoming a limited company in 1896; not only Weavings, but Hanley's City Brewery, Hilliards in Wallingford and Shillingfords at Bicester were acquired in just three years.

The tied houses belonging to Hunt, Edmunds in 1946. The map excludes outlets around Chipping Norton acquired through amalgamation with Hitchman's in 1925.

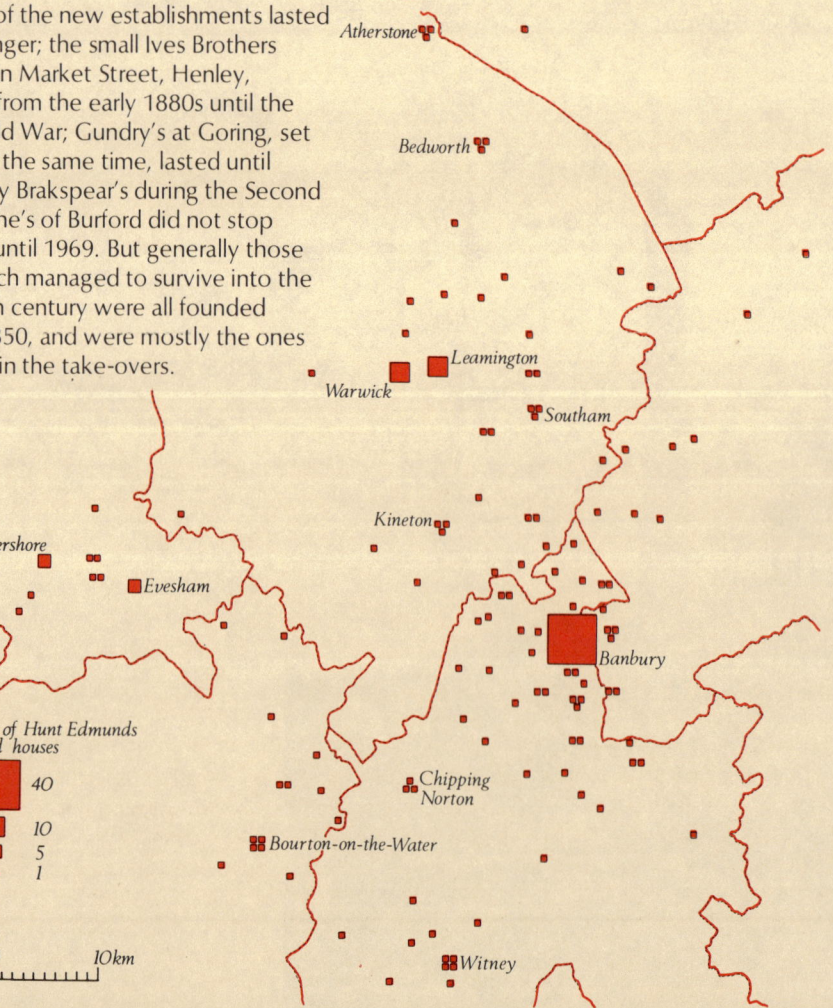

No. of Hunt Edmunds tied houses

40

10

5

1

0   10km

24

The Busy Bee, Brakspear's Foden steam lorry, delivering to the Little Angel at Remenham about 1900.

In Henley, Brakspear's bought out their last town rival, The Grey's Brewery, in 1898; Morlands took over other breweries in the town — Townsend's Tower Brewery, Child's Abbey Brewery and Belcher's Eagle Brewery — as well as Field's at Shillingford (1889). Hunt, Edmunds bought the Banbury Brewery 1879, the Sun Brewery in 1884 and their last rival in Banbury, Dunnell & Co. (successors to Austins), in 1918.

These competitive struggles went on against a background of older traditions. At the other end of the scale from the highly capitalised breweries there were still the small men and the brewing victuallers, scattered around the towns and villages. The tradition seems to have remained stronger in the west of the county and in the Vale of White Horse than in North or South Oxfordshire, or in the City. There were brewing publicans in Witney, Burford and Ducklington in the later 19th century, and the Haynes family operated a brewery at the Marlborough Arms in Woodstock which advertised 'sound home-brewed ales and stout; families and the trade supplied at short notice' in 1898. The Maltster and Shovel in Stonesfield was a well-known brewing house until 1939. Abingdon was a considerable centre for brewing publicans from the 1840s to 70s. One of these, Henry Mulcock of the Plumber's Arms was a man of considerable talents — in 1854 he advertised as Victualler, Plumber, Glazier, Paper Hanger, Brewer and Beer Retailer. But their production was a tiny part of the whole.

The big breweries were themselves diversifying at this time, not only increasing the range of their own beers, but becoming retailers of wines and spirits, as well as manufacturers of mineral waters and ginger beer. Here we can see a response to changing habits in drinking, and the brewer's determination to keep their share of the market. Increasingly, too, they were exploiting a new market for bottled beers to drink at home, and stressed both the family, and the healthiness of their beers, in their advertisements. All these developments required considerable expenditure on plant and premises.

Retailing was the key to success. The purpose of the takeovers of the 1880s and 1890s was almost always the acquisition of a rival's tied houses, to ensure a sale for the increased production at the home brewery made possible by new capital equipment. This fight for tied houses, which took place early in South Oxfordshire, was rather later in the north.

Hunt, Edmunds owned only one inn, in Banbury, until the 1870s. Then, having built up and modernised their brewing premises they turned their attention to the acquisition of a whole string of tied houses. Within seventy years their empire in six counties was considerable.

Such far flung outlets could, of course, only be supplied by modern transportation; earlier acquisitions of tied houses were limited by the capacity to deliver by horse and dray. Horses remained rather longer for town deliveries than for rural (until the 1940s in some cases) but already by the early 1900s, breweries with pubs in the countryside were investing in steam lorries. Between the wars, steam and the remaining drays were gradually replaced by motor lorries, making even more distant deliveries possible.

The take-overs of the 1880s and 90s were part of a process of consolidation by Oxfordshire breweries — a sign of health and expansion rather than decline. Most of the firms which had carried out the take-overs survived until the 1920s, when they began to be hit by a succession of very different take-overs. Some were local arrangements — in 1925, Hitchman's of Chipping Norton, for example, lost its independence to Hunt, Edmunds. But other take-overs involved breweries from outside the region: The Wallingford Brewery fell to Ushers of Trowbridge in the 1920s; Halls of Oxford was taken over by Allsop in 1926, and was thereby merged into Ind Coope in 1935. A fresh wave followed in the 60s — Wadworths of Devizes acquired Garne's Brewery in 1969, Clinch's Eagle Brewery was bought by Courage and Hunt, Edmunds themselves were taken over in 1967 by Mitchell and Butler. At all of these brewing ceased and the premises were used as bottling plants or stores before, in some cases, demolition.

Materials & Methods 2

The Oxfordshire Maltster: the rise of an industry

By the later sixteenth century the large brewing concerns in London were creating a considerable demand for malt from the surrounding counties. Oxfordshire, with its rich farmland for barley growing, was in a good position to help meet the need. Anthony Wood writing of Oxford in the 1650s observed 'About these times and before maltsters increased very much in Oxon, having now the number of 7 to one 20 or 18 years ago'. As well as growing in number, those engaged in malting were growing more inventive and more professional, particularly in the riverside towns. In 1673 Blome wrote that 'Henley had a considerable trade for malting, its inhabitants . . . gain a good livelihood by transporting of malt, wood and other goods to London, and in return bring such commodities as they and the inhabitants of the adjacent towns have need of . . . and its market is very considerable for corn, especially barley, which is brought there for their great malt trade'.

Many of the town's houses had malt kilns built into them or in the gardens and yards behind them, which attracted the attention of Dr Robert Plot in 1677.

There were plainly considerable changes taking place in the actual process of malting. By Plot's time the malt kiln had developed to the general form which it retained right through into our own century. He described and illustrated a kiln made at Burford by Valentine Strong 'an Ingenious Mason at Teynton, much after the manner of those of Brick, which for the Benefit of other *Counties* where they are not known, I have caused to be delineated . . .

These improved kilns were square in plan with the heat from a central fire being funnelled up the sloping sides of the kiln interior to the underside of a floor carried on four pillars; on the laths of this floor the barley was supported, spread out on a hair cloth. The cloth was eventually replaced by perforated square tiles, or by screens of wire mesh, but the form of the malthouse remained much the same for well over two hundred years. One of the earliest to survive in Oxfordshire is at the Garne's Brewery site in Burford, of late seventeenth or early eighteenth century date; the square kiln is at one end of a long building with an upper floor, plastered over, on which the steeped barley was spread. All the later malthouses were of this type. By the later nineteenth century some malthouses were very large indeed, with two or more growing floors and pairs of kilns.

The early centres for the malt trade were the riverside towns — Abingdon, Wallingford, Oxford and, above all, Henley. By the early eighteenth century, Burford, too, was an important malting centre, using wharves at Radcot Bridge to ship down river to London. Maltsters were wealthy and rose to positions of importance in these towns; in Oxford in the seventeenth century a succession of maltsters and brewers served as mayors or bailiffs as, in Abingdon, did the Bostock, Tesdale and Blacknall families. The growth of commercial brewing in the county from the 1700s further encouraged the malting industry and many of the brewers setting up in business in these years also had malting interests. With a ready availability of malt for purchase, domestic malting declined, so that by the end of the 1700s most household brewing, where it

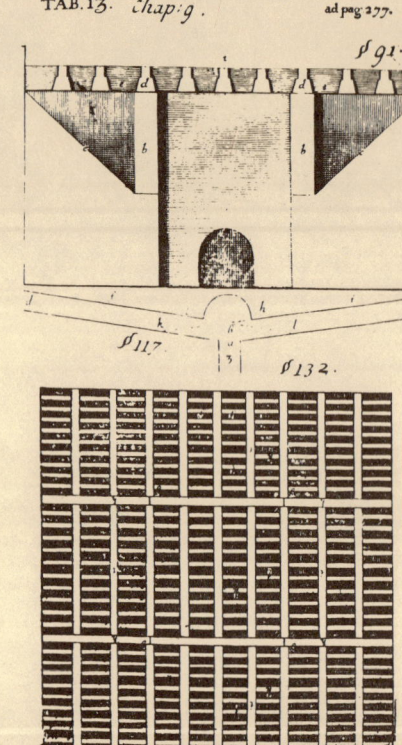

Valentine Strong's malthouse at Burford, section and plan, illustrated by Dr Plot in 1677.

survived, was using bought-in rather than home-produced malt. Some domestic malting, however, continued to a relatively late date: Solomon Goffe was advertising in 1761 — 'Earthen kilns for drying malt . . . are made, glazed and sold by Solomon Goffe of Leafield, near Burford, Oxfordshire, a Potter; N.B. They dry with less Fuel than Iron, and are much cheaper and more durable.'

Fuel was a constant pre-occupation of the maltster; coal was increasingly the normal kiln fuel from Plot's time onwards, especially as coke or anthracite. It gave a cleaner, less smokey, heat than wood, but it was expensive; and the importance of the Thames lay in allowing it to be brought in as well as the malt to be shipped out.

Improvements in river navigation greatly assisted the maltsters and in the 1770s 'since the making of the Isis navigable to barges to London . . . (Oxford) is become a place of great trade, principally in malt'. The opening of the Oxford Canal, connecting the Thames with the Midlands by the 1790s, also encouraged the growth of malting and brewing in the 18th and 19th centuries. Oxfordshire in 1801-2 was paying excise duty on nearly 520,000 bushels of malt, although its production was still being outstripped by Berkshire, Bedfordshire, Suffolk and Surrey. The half century after 1830 was the high point for the independent malting industry, and the malthouse had become a common industrial building in Witney, Burford, Banbury and Bicester, as well as in the riverside towns. Some were attached to breweries, but many more were independent. The particular growth was not in the older centres such as Henley, but in Witney and, especially, Banbury, with over forty maltsters recorded there between 1830 and 1890. Some of these were fairly small scale, but together they added up to a large production, only partly explained by the concentration of breweries in the town; of great

The maltsters at Hunt, Edmunds, Banbury 1872.

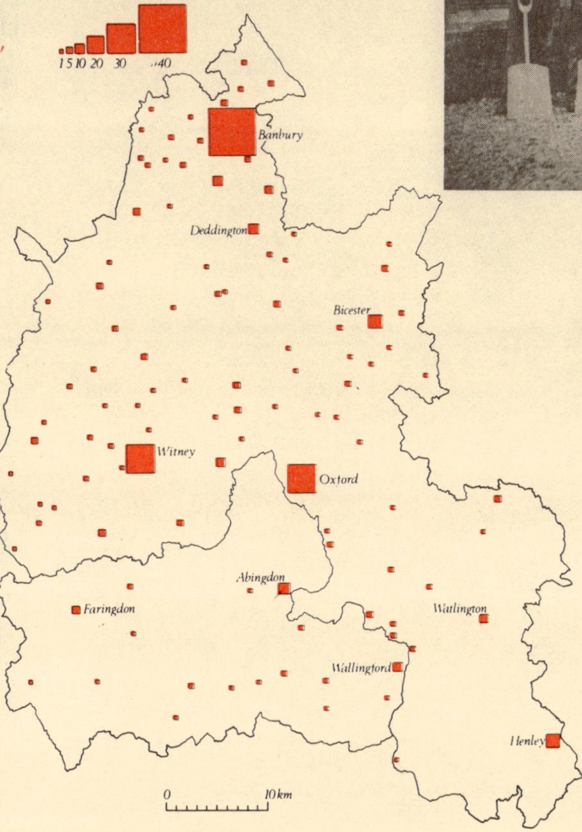

Numbers of maltsters operating in Oxfordshire between 1830 and 1880.

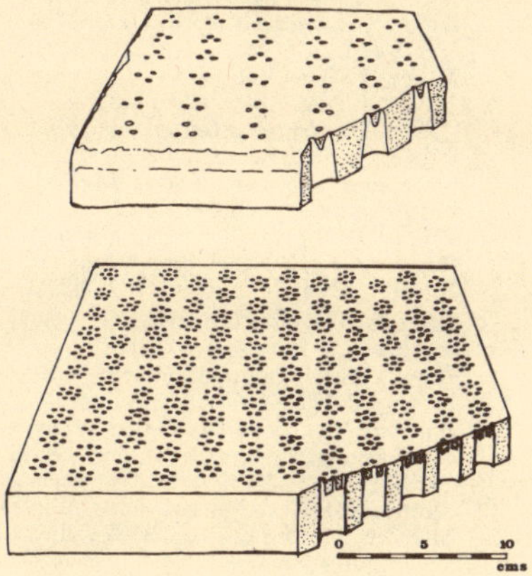

1 5 10 20 30 40

Banbury
Deddington
Bicester
Witney
Oxford
Abingdon
Faringdon
Watlington
Wallingford
Henley

0   10 km

(Below) Malt kiln tiles, eighteenth and nineteenth century, from Oxfordshire malthouses.

0   5   10
cms

Section through the malthouse on the Garne's Brewery site in Sheep Street, Burford.

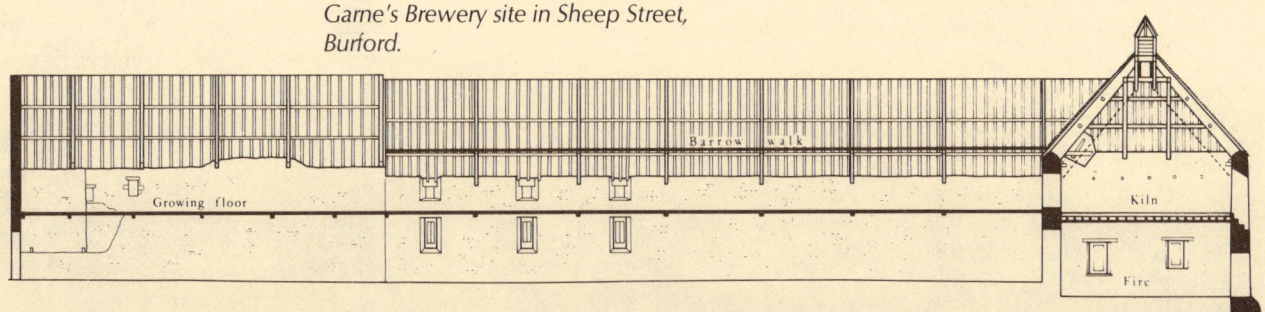

Growing floor

Barrow walk

Kiln

Fire

27

MALTSTERS.

Adkins W. Little Bourton, Banbury
Bateman C. Asthall, Burford, Oxford
Bayliss W. Fulbrook, Burford
Bennett N. Tadmarton, Banbury
Buller W. Hanwell, Banbury
Buller W. Neithrop, Banbury
Busby W. Swalcliffe, Banbury
Cherry J. Bloxham, Banbury
Claridge H. Chadlington, Enstone
Clinch J. W. & Sons, Eagle brewery,
    Witney
Cook H. Hanwell, Banbury
Coster H. Stadhampton, Wallingford
Dobson W. Gravel hill, Henley-on-Thames
Fidler J. Stonesfield, Woodstock
Field T. E. & Co. Shillingford, Wallingford
Field S. High street, Thame
Gardner J. Bodicot, Banbury
Gibbard G. Fingford, Bicester
Goodman W. North Aston, Deddington
Grisold R. Neithrop, Banbury
Hanley D. Iffley, Oxford
Harman J. N. St. John's road, Banbury
Harris J. Scotland, Hook Norton,
    Chipping Norton
Hatt R. Chalgrove, Tetsworth
Haynes Mrs. M. Westcot Barton, Oxford
Hiorns J. Sandford, Oxford
Hitchman & Co. West st. Chipping Norton
Huut & Edmunds, Bodicot, Banbury
Hunt & Edmunds, Fish street, Banbury
King W. Lower Heyford, Oxford
Merry J. L. Lower Cherwell st. Banbury
Miller W. New road, Oxford
Nalder J. Alvescot, Faringdon
Osborn W. Wardington, Banbury
Pankridge F. Bradwell, Lechlade
Pittman W. C. Goring, Reading
Porter W. Kencott, Lechlade
Prophett H. Sibford Ferris, Banbury
Reynolds T. H. Sheep street, Burford
Riggs T. B. Bell st. Henley-ou-Thames
Ring J. Wheatley, Oxford
Robinson J. Bloxham, Banbury
Rogers R. Bloxham, Banbury
Scroggs J. Horse fair, Deddington
Sheldon Jonathan, Eynsham, Oxford
Shillingford & Son, Eynsham, Oxford
Shillingford J. King's end, Bicester
Shuffrey Mrs. A. Market place, Witney
Spencer A. Shipton-under-Wychwood,
    Chipping Norton
Stevens J. Corn street, Witney
Sturch W. Market place, Deddington
Ward W. & Co. New road, Oxford
Ward H. Lower Cherwell st. Banbury
Ward H. Old wharf, Banbury
Waters G. S. Fringford, Bicester
Watts C. Lower Heyford, Oxford
Webb T. Sibford Gower, Banbury
Wing T. Islip, Oxford
Wycherly J. Adderbury, Oxford

Oxfordshire maltsters, listed in the Post Office Directory, 1864. Most of them at this date were still independent operators.

importance also were the good transport links with the cities of the Midlands — Birmingham and Coventry, with their own demands for good quality malt. But the position of the independent maltster was threatened by the success of the brewers who were able to raise capital, buy out their competitors and reorganize their breweries. Malt, as their basic raw material, was expensive and the brewers preferred to control its production rather than rely on the vagaries, of price and quality, of independent supply. As premises were re-organized or rebuilt, a malthouse was often added. Hunt, Edmunds put up their enormous malthouse in Banbury in 1866, the largest single building in the town, and most of the other breweries had built their own maltings by the early years of this century. The smaller malthouses, tucked away behind the houses of market towns, fell into disuse or were converted for other purposes. Ironically, these brewery maltings were themselves relatively short lived. By the middle of our own century, malting on site was no longer economical and the breweries once again resorted to outside suppliers. Today, although the number of malthouses is reduced to two, Oxfordshire remains an important centre of malting. The huge Associated British Maltsters plant at Wallingford, built in the 1960s, produces malt in a series of sophisticated industrial processes which, however, remain in essence the same as those carried out in the traditional malthouse. The majority of the malt goes to supply the brewing industry, locally and nationally, as in the past, but a considerable export trade has now been built up. A second large ABM maltings in Abingdon, on the old Vineyard site, has recently been acquired by the Watney Mann and Trueman group for supplying their breweries.

Brakspear's great malthouse in New Street, Henley, about 1900: the exterior, the kiln furnace, and one of the growing floors.

The End of the Mystery: Science and Invention in Brewing

The development which turned the common brewer of the eighteenth century into the great commercial brewery of the nineteenth was accompanied by three other processes — increasing scientific control of the 'art or mystery' of brewing, the introduction of improved and more efficient plant and an ever growing range of brews to suit all tastes. Throughout the 1700s there were attempts, particularly amongst the London breweries, to understand what actually happened during the brewing process, but much of brewing remained a hit and miss affair, which relied on accumulated experience rather than scientific knowledge, well into the nineteenth century. The main problem was of measurement, particularly of temperature, which was crucial in mashing and in fermentation, and of the 'strength' of the brew, on which its price was based. A thermometer was first used by a London brewer in the 1750s but they did not come into common use until the 1780s; at about the same time experiments were still in hand to produce a reliable hydrometer (or saccharometer, as it was called) to measure the specific gravity of the beer. These inventions were taken up by enterprising brewers outside the capital; Robert Brakspear had both, though he had problems with his saccharometer in 1786 — 'the preceeding gravities are by no means to be relied on, as, from a non acquaintance with several incidents in the use of the Instrument . . . use was constantly liable to error'. A third invention, the attemperator, designed to reduce the temperature in the mashing and fermenting vessels and so allow summer brewing, was adopted more slowly; Brakspear, for instance, did not have any such equipment, and it was only in the following century that refrigeration was introduced locally.

The other great eighteenth century innovation, the steam engine, was only worthwhile for brewing on a scale beyond that of most Oxfordshire brewers until the later nineteenth century. Until then the horse-mill and the horse-pump had to serve. There was a horse-mill at Charles Moore's brewery in St. Aldates in 1765, when it was destroyed in a violent thunderstorm. A plan of Brakspear's in 1836 shows the millhouse for the horse engine; a steam engine was not installed until 1865. There are references to millhouses in advertisements for the sale or letting of brewing premises in the eighteenth century.

Such improvements as there were concentrated on the vessels themselves, the piping which connected them and the pumps which supplied the water (or liquor as it is always called in brewing) and moved it round the sequence of processes. Of particular importance were the deep wells which supplied water to the premises; every succesful brewery required constant and dependable supplies of good pure water.

Advertisement in Jackson's Oxford Journal, 1814, detailing the equipment of a common brewer's establishment in Banbury. Most of the work of a brewery at this date would still have been done by hand.

Only with the expansion and capitalisation of Oxfordshire's breweries in the second half of the nineteenth century did the range of available improvements and new machinery begin to be introduced — steam power, cast iron vessels, proper refrigeration, new types of mash tuns with revolving spargers to

Title, in Robert Brakspear's hand, of one of the careful records which he kept of his experiments in brewing, 1790s.

Hydrometric

Observations & Experiments

The Hook Norton Brewery — exterior, diagrammatic section and the last stage of the process, fermentation.

Cold Liquor Tank

Grist Mill

Flat Cooler

Refrigerator

Hot Liquor Tank

Grist Hopper

Mash Tun   Mash Tun

Sweet Wort Taps

Fermenting Tuns

Copper

Hop Back

Steam Engine

Storage Tank

Casking & Bottling

sprinkle the mash and extract the maximum from the malt, new machines for screening the malt and crushing it between steel rollers to produce grist for the mash tun. Hunt, Edmunds, as we have seen, were installing these improvements one by one in the 1850s and 60s. Those breweries which opted for wholesale redevelopment acquired them all at once in the new and distinctive brewing towers. Gravity had for long been used in moving the brew; the gravitational tower utilized it to the maximum and reduced the need to pump to a single operation — the initial movement of liquor up to the top of the tower. The brewery at Hook Norton (actually a semi-gravitational brewery in that two pumping operations are necessary) remains a good example of the principle in action: the actual processes are the same in any traditional brewing operation. Steam power pumps the water from deep wells up to the *cold liquor tanks* at the very top of the tower. The same power hoists the sacked malt up to the malt store from where it can be carried to the *grist mill* for crushing. The liquor flows down to be heated in the *hot liquor tank* before mixing with the malt from the *grist hopper* in the *mash tun*. Mashing takes place at about 150°F, and the starch in the malt is converted into

soluble sugars; much of the character of the beer is determined by the temperature of the mash. After *sparging* — sprinkling with more hot liquor — the resulting *sweet wort* is run off. The spent malt is sold for cattle feed. The wort flows into the *copper* where it is boiled with hops, imparting the oils and resins which give flavour and preservative qualities. After running into the *hop back* the wort is filtered through the spent hops (which become a useful fertilizer for market gardeners).

The second pumping now takes place as the wort is pumped back up to the top of the tower into a large flat copper *cooler*. Louvres in the roof assist an initial cooling before the wort is run through a refrigerating plant, exchanging its heat with a counter flow of cold water, into the *fermenting tuns* where yeast is added to begin the process of fermentation. Up to this point the process has taken a few hours, but fermentation is carried on over four or five days, as the yeast multiplies and the sugar in the wort is converted to alcohol. The temperature is critical and is controlled by cooling coils within the vessels. When the fermenting is complete, the beer (as it now is) is allowed to rest before being ready for *racking* into casks or bottling tank.

Genuine Ales and Porter: later varieties of beer

A number of factors can influence the taste and appearance of the brew. The degree of kilning of the malt (less heat for a paler, lighter brew, more for a darker beer with a fuller flavour), the chemical composition of the liquor, the temperature and the completeness of mashing, the type of hops used, the length and temperature of fermentation, all have effects on the final product. As understanding of the brewing process grew, it was possible for the brewer to introduce more refinements and develop new types of beer with some confidence that they would turn out how he wanted them.

The original distinction between ale (cervisia —the unhopped brew) and beer (birra — with the addition of hops) soon became confused by usage. The terms remained but the meaning attached to them changed. Because hops were first used in London, beer was thought of as the city drink, ale as what was made in the more conservative country areas. When the London breweries after the 1720s developed a new type of drink, porter — a dark strong brew which kept well — it was natural to refer to it as beer; the lighter, clearer brews of the provinces were still called 'ales', even though by now they were hopped. As the darker brews spread outside London, the distinction was retained — the Banbury Brewery Company in 1865 were still advertising themselves as 'Ale and Porter Brewers'. Today the distinction has largely disappeared in general use; beer is now a general term covering all brewed liquor, but ale still means a paler drink. Porter covered what the brewers referred to as 'mild', as well as stout. As its fame spread, some provincial brewers felt

obliged to develop their own variety. Robert Brakspear, who had experimented with making a mild in the 1780s, began to brew an amber porter in 1797 using the local amber malts. In the following years he was also making three kinds of brew: a strong, an amber strong and a weaker 'small' beer.

Tastes from the early nineteenth century were anyway moving away from the thicker darker beers towards the lighter. India Pale Ale, developed for the export trade, was first brewed in London in the later 1700s but rapidly gained a popularity at home, particularly among the middle and upper classes; it was light, sparkling and bitter. Oxfordshire breweries continued to brew both varieties — ales and stouts — as their advertisements show. The lighter beers were suitable for 'family' use and at the table; the stouts were particularly valuable for invalids. The stronger the beer, the more expensive it was. Towards the end of the century bottled beers were becoming available and special brews were developed for bottling. The X rating system was used to denote the strength and quality of the beers, with gradings from X to XXXX. The same pattern has continued to the present day, with the Oxfordshire breweries each making a range of beers, draught and bottled. In addition to their regular output of draught bitters and milds, with bottled ales and stout, some produce special stronger brews for the winter (old ales, in that they are matured for longer than normal) and Celebration Ales to mark important national and local events.

Page from the account book of Thomas Banks at the Red Lion, Steeple Aston, recording deliveries from Hall's of Oxford, 1872.

Advertisement in Jackson's Oxford Journal, 1905.

Oxfordshire Breweries Today

By 1970, Oxfordshire's stock of working breweries was reduced to four. Since then, however, a renewal of interest in traditionally brewed beers, encouraged by the Campaign for Real Ale, has revived brewing at almost every level: domestic brewing is once again widespread, some publicans are once more beginning to brew on the premises, and small independent brewers are beginning to appear — one brewing in the malthouse of Clinch's old brewery in Witney. And the four surviving commercial breweries — more than in many counties — are again finding an interested and appreciative market to help assure their future. Brewing, unlike many of Oxfordshire's ancient trades, is once again flourishing; this booklet concludes with a brief survey of these four survivors and one which did not survive, but which has been, at least partially, revived.

Morland's of Abingdon

The remote village of West Ilsley in the Berkshire Downs was the original home of the Morland family brewing business. John Morland, yeoman, bought West Ilsley House, 'including the malthouse' in 1711; his son, Benjamin, built a new brewhouse, and his grandson William continued in the trade. He was the first Morland to describe himself as Brewer rather than Yeoman in the local records. The West Ilsley brewery, which included a cooperage, was one of two in the village, from which 'Barrell Court' was named.

The Morland family was a large one. Some went into law and public service; Henry Robert (1716-1797) and his son George (1763-1804) were artists, a connection commemorated in the Company's logo. William successfully built up the brewing business in West Ilsley. One of his younger sons, Benjamin, moved to Abingdon to practice law (1791), but when his nephew died childless, it was Benjamin's son Edward Henry who inherited the West Ilsley brewery (1855) and acquired the Eagle Brewery, Abingdon in 1861 (the site of the present Brewery). Five years later, in 1866, Edward acquired the Abbey Brewery in Abingdon through the Trustees of Mary Spenlove, the daughter of Susanna Morland, his aunt, who had married into the Spenlove brewing family of Abingdon. In this short time, the independent country brewer had turned Victorian capitalist manager. Edward concentrated all the business at the Eagle Brewery in Abingdon, and brewing ceased at West Ilsley and the Abbey. Other independent breweries were acquired — Saxby's Brewery in Stert Street, Abingdon and Field and Sons of Shillingford (1889).

A new brewery, still in use today, was built on the site of the Eagle Brewery in 1911/12. Water was pumped from wells on the premises by a steam engine. There was an old malthouse (since demolished) and a new malthouse was built in 1906, but after malting ceased, it was used for other purposes including the present offices. Ock Lea House still survives from the Eagle Brewery days.

The early 20th century saw further amalgamations, with the Wantage Brewery Co., (1920), Hewitt & Co. Ltd., of Waltham St. Lawrence, Dymore-Brown & Son, Reading, Fergusons Ltd. of Reading and Belcher and Habgood, Abingdon (1927-1928). These acquisitions secured nearly 300 tied public houses, and retail wine and spirit businesses for the Company. A mineral water business was established at the Eagle Brewery premises and mineral water production continues to this day.

One factor enabling such amalgamation was the change from horse-drawn transport to steam and later motor vehicles. Horse-drawn drays were kept, however, for local deliveries and enjoyed a revival during World War II; four were kept on at Morland's until 1950. Early salesmen, known as outriders, used a pony and trap, then motor-cycles with sidecars.

Morland's tied houses are mostly in Oxfordshire, Berkshire and the Thames and Kennet Valleys. Draught beers are Bitter, Best Bitter and Mild. Special bottled beers have been brewed for the MG Jubilee (Old Speckled Hen) 1979; The Royal Jubilee (1977) and the Royal Wedding (1981).

Delivering to the George & Dragon, Abingdon c. 1900.

Part of the Morland's motor lorry fleet, 1948.

W. H. Brakspear & Sons; The Henley Brewery.

Born in Faringdon in 1750, Robert Brakspear by the age of nineteen was landlord of the Cross Keys Inn at Witney. He stayed there for ten years, brewing for himself and for sale to other publicans in the town. His uncle, Richard Hayward, ran a brewery and malthouse in Bell Street, Henley; in 1779 Brakspear moved there and two years later became a partner in the brewery. On Hayward's death in 1797 his half share passed to Brakspear, who was able to buy out the remaining partner in 1803 and thus become sole proprietor.

The brewery in these years was small by national standards; it produced less than 4,500 barrels in 1784-5 when the big London breweries were turning out 100,000 barrels each. Its successful management, however, demanded great skill and financial sense. Hops and malt were expensive, and their purchase and storage needed careful judgement and planning; the brewing of the beer itself was a process still only imperfectly understood in Brakspear's day, and he set about improving his own understanding of it, taking scientific measurements and keeping a detailed record of each brew in books of 'Practical Notes'. Between 1795 and 1811 about 105 brewings were taking place each year, of three types of beer — a strong, an amber strong and a weak 'small' beer. Brakspear also experimented with making an amber porter. Competition between breweries was increasing, particularly through the acquisition of tied houses

and by 1812 Brakspear had thirty four such houses; his main local competitors were Simonds of Reading, Haywards of Watlington, and Appleton and Shaw, brewers in New Street, Henley. In 1812, the year of his death, Robert Brakspear negotiated the amalgamation of his own company with Appleton and Shaw. Soon afterwards the old Bell Street Brewery was closed, and all activity concentrated on the New Street site. Robert's son, William Henry Brakspear, inherited his father's good luck and energy. He became a partner in 1825, and by 1848 a Brakspear was once again sole proprietor. During his 57 years at the brewery, W. H. Brakspear worked tirelessly to expand the company. More beerhouses were acquired and malthouses taken over. Production increased to serve the new outlets, from 9,000 barrels a year in 1838 to 14,300 in 1882. His sons, Archibald and George were taken into partnership, and after their father's death in 1882 steered the company successfully through the difficult years of the late century. They introduced improvements to their houses and to the brewery itself — a new cooper's shop in 1886, a new brewhouse in 1892 — though there was no complete rebuilding as at some local breweries. In 1896 Brakspear's bought out and closed down their main local rival, The Grey's Brewery in Henley. The capital to do this could only be raised by establishing the firm as a limited company; successive members of the family have continued to serve as chairman.

In this century, Brakspear's has managed to retain its independence, gradually buying out all its remaining local competitors; the last was Gundry's Goring Brewery in 1941. Methods were improved, particularly of transport to the extensive collection of

tied houses. Today Brakspear's is flourishing. By 1979, their bicentenary year, production was over 30,000 barrels a year and their range of beers — a dark mellow Old, a dark sweet mild and two bitters — was being supplied to 130 tied houses, as well as some free houses, in the towns and villages of South Oxfordshire.

Robert Brakspear

The Brewery Yard, about 1900.

Hook Norton Brewery

The Hook Norton Brewery Company, one of only twenty five wholly independent breweries remaining in the country, has successfully withstood the pressures of a contracting industry. By adapting its production to meet the changing times, brewing has continued unhindered for 137 years, under the guidance of the same family.

The Hook Norton Brewery was begun by John Harris, whose family were farmers in Chilson. Harris later moved to Hook Norton, renting a 52 acre farm from John Parish in the Scotland End area of the village. The farm had a tradition of producing malt for village use and as early as 1847 Harris established himself as a farmer and maltster. In September 1852 he purchased the Scotland End site for £350.

By 1856 brewing records show that he was brewing beer commercially and by 1872 a new purpose built brewery became a necessity. Henry Pontifex, a London Architect and Brewery Consultant, was engaged to draw up plans. Harris's business relied on the extensive network of private outlets built up in the area, but in 1869 he made a tentative entry into the tied house trade, purchasing the Pear Tree Beerhouse in Hook Norton for £210. By the end of the nineteenth century, Harris's Brewery was supplying twelve different beers, to meet the demand created by the private trade and a growing tied house trade, which supplied customers as far afield as Birmingham, Witney and Byfield.

The new tower brewery at Hook Norton, shown in an advertising poster, early twentieth century.

John Harris died in 1887, leaving the business to his son John Henry and nephew Alban Clarke. Under new, dynamic management the brewery entered a boom period, which saw the acquisition of further tied houses and culminated in a massive rebuilding programme involving new stables, offices and a semi-gravitational tower brewery between 1899 and 1901, designed by London brewery architect, William Bradford. In 1901, during the rebuilding programme, the Harris family brewery became a limited company, known as The Hook Norton Brewery Company.

The First World War brought changes to the brewery. The malting of barley and the private trade became casualties of Government restrictions and ceased. The securing of a Government licence in 1918 to supply Coventry Working Men's Clubs provided a life-line, through which developed a major part of the brewery's trade.

In May 1917 Alban Clarke died after a cycling accident. His son Bill, not old enough to join the Company, remained at school, while Percy Flick, who joined the firm some years earlier, became Managing Director.

The years following the First World War were difficult ones. It was uncertain if the brewery would survive. By 1928 Flick's policies had piloted the brewery through its most difficult years and Bill Clarke began the long, distinguished connection with the Company that was to span 54 years.

The Second War brought a boom that came as a sharp contrast to the lean inter-war years. With demand exceeding output, the brewery worked on, overcoming mechanical failures and Government restrictions, to produce all the beer it could sell. It was not until after the 1951 election that restrictions were lifted and normal business was once again possible.

Bill Clarke was actively concerned with the running of the brewery until his death in January 1982. He was succeeded as Managing Director by his son, David, who joined the Company in 1960, being the fourth generation of the family involved in running the business. Since 1960 the yearly output has doubled, so that today the Hook Norton Brewery produces 22,000 barrels a year — over six million pints — to supply its 34 tied houses, the Coventry Clubs and the demand from free trade outlets. The brewery no longer produces twelve different beers, but its present range of Best Bitter, Mild and Old Hookey are available within fifty miles of Hook Norton.

Morrell's Brewery.

Mark Morrell and his son James entered the brewing business in the late eighteenth century as partners of the Tawneys, an old-established Oxford brewing family, to whom they were related by marriage. It would seem that the brewery in St. Thomas's High Street was established in 1782 on the site which had already been used for brewing for some two hundred years. The brewery stretched along the west bank of Wareham Stream, a back-stream of the Thames.

Upon the death of James Morrell in 1855 the business passed to his son, also named James, and continued to be managed directly by the family until 1863, after which it was administered for them by trustees.

Following a major re-fit of the brewery in about 1896 it was equipped with two large boiling coppers — one open (160 barrels capacity) for the production of bitter, and the other closed for the brewing of stout. Two mash tuns gave a working capacity of up to 2,500 barrels per week. The brewery incorporated large bottling stores, where the beers were bottled direct from the cask, a spacious cask washing shed, offices, laboratory and stabling. Power was provided by a combination of steam engines and a water wheel in Wareham Stream, which still survives, having been restored as part of the bicentenary celebrations.

Morrell's, like Hall's was an important employer and significant landowner in West Oxford. In addition to the many tied houses owned by Morrell's they owned other properties which they leased to brewery employees. Many of the houses in Lower Fisher Row were owned by Morrell's and were leased to their humbler employees for as little as two shillings a week during the mid nineteenth century. In the 1860s even the brewery manager Thomas Sherwood was living in brewery-owned property; he and his family lived in Richard Tawney's old house almost opposite the brewery.

Morrell's maintained a sizeable fleet of brewery drays for local deliveries of their beer; like Hall's, they also despatched large shipments by river transport. During the 1860s-1870s the local trade directories list an address for Morrell's at The Wharf, near Folly Bridge.

During the early years of this century Morrell's publicity laid much emphasis on the fact that their beer was solely the product of malt and hops. A circular letter put out by the brewery in 1901 stressed that 'the recent cases of poisoning in the Midlands show what dangers may be encountered in drinking beer brewed from a cheap form of sugar'. Since 1943 Morrell's has been run as a private limited liability company under the control of the Morrell family. The equipment of the present-day brewery (some modern, some dating from 1901) operates behind the traditional exterior of the original brewery site; the entrance to the Lion Brewery and its offices is still through the imposing late nineteenth century cast iron gateway, dominated by a pair of rampant lions. Still independent, Morrell's Brewery Ltd. owns 140 public houses in the Oxford area.

The Morrells are an excellent example of the prosperity and position which could be achieved by a successful brewing family. One branch, founded by James Morrell (1739-1807) became prominent in local administrative and legal affairs. Two of his descendants married the daughters of Oxford college presidents, and in the early years of this century Philip Morrell, M.P. for South Oxfordshire, and his wife, Lady Ottoline, regularly entertained leading literary figures of the day at Garsington Manor. The brewing branch of the family, founded by James' brother Mark, also prospered; his son acquired Headington Hill Hall by 1831 and the house was rebuilt in 1856-58; it remained in the family, the largest private house in Oxford, until 1953.

Entrance to Morrell's Lion Brewery, Oxford, possibly photographed by Henry Taunt, late nineteenth century. (Oxfordshire County Libraries).

Hall's Brewery, Oxford

In 1795 William Hall purchased the 'Swan's Nest Brewery' (later the Swan Brewery) from Sir John Treacher, one time alderman and mayor of Oxford. The brewery, situated on a narrow strip of land between two channels of the Thames in St. Thomas's parish, was in existence as early as 1718. By 1835 William Hall was in partnership with the Tawney family who had been involved in the brewing industry in Oxford since the mid eighteenth century; from 1837 Henry Hall headed the firm.

In 1896 the brewery was converted into a company under the name of Hall's Oxford Brewery Ltd. In 1897 it took over two other Oxford breweries — the St. Clement's Brewery (Wootten's) and the Eagle Steam Brewery (Weaving's) in Park End Street. The following year saw the addition of Hilliard's of Wallingford, Shillingford's of Bicester and Hanley's City Brewery, Oxford.

The intention behind this spate of take-overs appears to have been to increase the number of tied houses attached to the brewery rather than to build upon going concerns. In Oxford the Eagle Brewery, partially rebuilt after a fire in 1894, was principally used for bottling. Here the buildings followed a fairly conventional brewery layout with cooperage, blacksmiths and stables attached. The main entrance in Park End Street was through an impressive cast-iron gateway crowned with an eagle; gas lamps were mounted on the pillars on either side. The main brewery operation was at the City Brewery.

Road and river were initially used by the brewery to deliver their beers, but the connection of Oxford to the railway network in 1851 greatly increased the speed of deliveries outside the locality. Local deliveries were carried out by a fleet of over sixty brewery drays of various kinds pulled by one to three horses. The brewery took considerable pride in this fleet and put it to good use for publicity purposes. Prior to the First World War the Hall's drays processed around Oxford as part of the annual May Day festivities, having first drawn up for inspection in St. Giles.

Hall's enamelled advertising signs in the 1880s were advertising the free delivery of crates of Pale Ale (1/- per gallon) to any railway station; similarly, empty casks could be returned free of charge to the brewery by rail or carrier. Large consignments were usually sent by river; a thousand casks of beer were despatched by Halls to London Docks in November 1871.

Procession of Hall's Brewery drays at the Plain, Oxford, May Morning, 1912. (Taunt photo, Oxfordshire County Libraries).

Hall's malthouse was in Beckett Street to the west of the Eagle Brewery; prior to the 1896 takeover this had been Hanley's maltings. In 1902 the malthouse was rebuilt following a £20,000 fire. The site is now occupied by the GPO sorting office.

A takeover by Allsopps in 1926 closed this chapter in the history of brewing in Oxford. The City Brewery closed (it is now the Oxford Museum of Modern Art) and the Head Office moved to the Eagle Brewery where bottling continued. Allsopps were subsequently acquired by Ind Coope, now part of Allied Breweries.

The ancient name of Halls, however, unlike Oxfordshire's other vanished breweries, has not been allowed to die. The revival of consumer interest in traditionally brewed beers persuaded Allied in 1980 to establish a new company, Hall's Oxford and West Brewery Co. Ltd. with headquarters at the Eagle Brewery. The beer sold under the Halls trade mark is now brewed in Burton but is supplied to a large number of the old Hall's tied houses in the county and further afield. More recently, in 1984, the company has embarked on a development which draws on an even older tradition; at the old Red Lion in Gloucester Green, Oxford, a brewhouse and bakehouse, with public house attached, have been set up. Four beers are brewed on the premises — a best, a porter, and two brews called "Tapper" and "Oxbow" — and served over the counter as in the days of the old Oxford alehouse brewer.

Alderman William Hall, a caricature of 1807 by Robert Dighton. (Bodleian, G. A. Oxon a80 page 24).